Two Park Street

BY PAUL BROOKS

ROADLESS AREA

THE PURSUIT OF WILDERNESS

THE HOUSE OF LIFE
Rachel Carson at Work

THE VIEW FROM LINCOLN HILL

SPEAKING FOR NATURE

THE OLD MANSE

TWO PARK STREET
A Publishing Memoir

Two
Park Street

A Publishing Memoir

Paul Brooks

with drawings by the author

BOSTON

HOUGHTON MIFFLIN COMPANY

1986

Library of Congress Cataloging-in-Publication Data

Brooks, Paul.
Two Park Street.

1. Brooks, Paul. 2. Houghton Mifflin Company —
History. 3. Publishers and publishing — Massachusetts —
Boston — History — 20th century. 4. Publishers and
publishing — United States — Biography. 5. Editors —
United States — Biography. I. Title.
z473.B82A3 1986 070.4'09744'61 86-10479
ISBN 0-395-37774-9

Printed in the United States of America

A 10 9 8 7 6 5 4 3 2 1

To the Park Street family

THEN AND NOW

Contents

Author's Note

NEITHER AUTOBIOGRAPHY NOR FORMAL HISTORY, this memoir recalls some aspects of book publishing as seen from Houghton Mifflin's offices on Park Street, beginning at a time when canvas awnings still shaded the tall windows facing the Common; when on spring mornings a distinguished editor and the chairman of the Massachusetts Audubon Society (whose office I temporarily shared) would conscientiously scout the sidewalk below to make certain that the coast was clear before he lowered the awning and released the fresh pigeon egg it invariably contained. Or was he seeking a target? I never dared ask.

Most of these chapters deal with the period from the early nineteen thirties through the sixties — a time when book publishing was as much a profession as a business, with the personal relation between writer and editor at its core.

With the communications industry getting ever larger and more complex, it is sometimes all but forgotten that the seed of the whole literary business is a writer with an idea. The book itself, the magazine and newspaper serialization, the motion picture, the paperback reprint, the television serial, the value of the publisher's stock — they all stem from the original idea and its successful execution.

Success, however, cannot always be judged by quick return on the invested dollar. Many of the titles that make up a publisher's backlist — the lifeblood of the business — would never have seen the light of day if their authors' first books had been required to show an immediate profit. But long-term predictions are difficult. Shortly after Houghton Mifflin Company "went public" in 1967, members of the executive committee were invited to a Wall Street luncheon with a number of stock analysts and investment bankers. They wanted to know what new books we would publish and what earnings we projected over the next five years. When it came my turn to speak for the Trade Department, I was stumped. Who knows? I did say, quite truthfully, that I had recently dined in San Francisco's Chinatown and had been given a fortune cookie that read: "You are about to be transferred to a distant branch office, with a large raise in salary." I went on to mention a few promising books we had currently in the works and then concluded, somewhat sententiously, that all we could do was to try to get the best cookies and let the fortunes take care of themselves.

Other products bring more predictable returns. One can sympathize with the efficient and well-organized Houghton Mifflin salesman who decided to change jobs, from selling books to selling vitaminized hog feed. The worth of the product was easier to quantify, and the taste of the consumer far less fickle.

Such pattern as these memoirs may have is based on subject rather than on strict chronology. For example, I first met Roger Tory Peterson in 1933, but the story of the Field Guide series continues to this day. Similarly, the Houghton Mifflin Literary Fellowship plan, initiated two years later, is still alive and flourishing.

Since more than three thousand books must have been published by the Trade Department during my time, I can mention only a tiny proportion of the titles and authors in each category. These are representative of scores of others equally worth remembering.

The scope of this book is limited. It deals solely with "trade" — as differentiated from "educational" — publishing (i.e., with the books you find in the bookstores), principally with adult titles, and in large part with the editorial side of the business. It is confined to one small segment of a long tradition.

I

Beginnings

I AM OFTEN ASKED, "How does one get into the publishing business?" How indeed. My own experience is of little help. It all began rather informally during a convivial dinner at the *Harvard Lampoon*, of which I was president. In the spring of 1931 the country was wallowing in the depths of the Great Depression. But one member of our group, Roger L. Scaife, a *Lampoon* graduate trustee and a top executive of Houghton Mifflin Company, was, at that moment, anything but depressed. Inexplicably, he offered me a job on graduation. Not to seem too eager, I paused for perhaps ten seconds before accepting. Next morning, I wondered whether he would remember. In due course came a letter offering me a position as an apprentice in the trade editorial department at fifteen dollars a week.

The following August, after marriage and a honeymoon, I entered Two Park Street for the first time. I had been instructed to be in Mr. Scaife's office at nine o'clock sharp. So I waited nervously on a hard sofa until Mr. S. appeared at nine-thirty, his secretary meanwhile looking at me from time to time with justified skepticism. Stepping in jauntily, he sat down at a small antique desk which had once belonged to Thomas Bailey Aldrich — whose biography had been written by Scaife's partner, Ferris Greenslet, chief editor of the Trade Department. The desk was quite hopeless to work at, but I'm sure Mr. Scaife liked the literary associations. So, after a brisk greeting, he pulled out the lower drawer of the desk and rested one of his feet on it, thus acquiring some appearance of informal comfort. What he had to say I can't recall, but he probably explained, among other things, his system for summoning subordinates: a buzzer with a code signal for each member of the department. This, I later suspected, served also as a means of creating an interruption on a dull day when he found it difficult to seem busy.

I was then ushered into a small office with two roll-top desks. The desk nearest the window, overlooking Boston Common, was occupied by a neatly dressed, slightly formal gentleman with white hair and clipped mustache, who greeted me with great civility, though I'm sure that this sudden sharing of his office with an inexperienced youngster could not have been welcome. I was given a typescript to read and a lot of HMCo stationery for which I had no use whatever. The day passed slowly, with the Park Street Church on the corner striking the quarter hours. Meanwhile my roommate, Francis H. Allen, a distinguished ornithologist (which I was not aware of at the time), having relieved our awning of its pigeon egg, dictated letter after letter about a Marbled Godwit (a handsome shorebird; see page 57) that he had seen on Cape Cod during the weekend — the first recorded in Massachusetts since 1888. This I found somewhat puzzling. But I guess he felt that he had earned a day off from publishing routine. He was an independent soul of considerable dignity. The story goes that on *his* first day at Houghton Mifflin (he came there straight from high school) he was just mounting the front steps when Mr. Mifflin rode up on his horse, having come from the Riverside Press in Cambridge. Spotting young Allen, he called out, "Here, boy, hold my horse!" "Sir," replied Allen, "I was hired as an office boy, not as a hostler," and continued up the steps. Some forty years later FHA, by then a senior editor, would be largely responsible for HMCo's acceptance of Roger Tory Peterson's *A Field Guide to the Birds*, which — with the series that followed — has earned millions for the firm.

At last the clock of the Park Street Church struck half-past twelve, and the seemingly interminable morning was at an end. With extraordinary graciousness, Mr. Scaife had invited me to lunch with him, that first day, at the Union Club: a bowl of crackers and milk, with blueberries. After lunch, as we were leaving the Club, the corporate image so pleasantly projected by my host became slightly tarnished. In the corridor we met HMCo's treasurer, James Duncan Phillips. I was duly introduced and held out my hand. There was no response, so I nervously put it back where it came from. A snort from the treasurer: "Huh! Another one of those young puppies!" and he turned on his heel.

My arrival at Two Park Street was barely noticed, but not quite unheralded. Years later I came across in an old file a memorandum from Mr. Scaife to his fellow directors, clipped to an account in the *Boston Evening Transcript* of the 1931 Harvard Commencement exercises. (In those days no event — including birth, marriage, and death — was considered wholly legitimate without a *Transcript* notice.) Having been Class Orator, I was given a good deal of space. By circulating this document, my sponsor was doubtless seeking to justify his impulsive behavior in adding another body — even at fifteen dollars a week — to the department payroll in such parlous times.

My only experience with publishing, aside from the *Lampoon*, was a pocket-size volume of lighthearted verse about Harvard professors, entitled *Mondays at Nine*, which sold pretty well around Harvard Square.

Now, little by little, I acquired some idea of what HMCo published, and why. The names of many writers then supporting the Trade Department still ring a clear, if distant, bell. One whom I had celebrated in verse was John Livingston Lowes, star of the English Department and author of the famous *Road to Xanadu*. He had been a frequent guest at dinner in Lampy's Elizabethan hall. Small of stature, with booming voice, he would make his points by slashing the air with a vertical motion of his forefinger, endangering the waistcoat buttons of his interlocutor as he sought to clinch his argument — and giving us a feeling for literature worth a course of formal lectures.

Other authors on the current publication lists I knew only by name or anecdote. One was Amy Lowell, imagist poet and biographer of John Keats, about whom Mr. Greenslet (a young employee who addressed him as "Ferris" soon sought his fortune elsewhere) would fondly reminisce. There was pathos in his recollection of how she would drape all the mirrors in her house lest she catch a glimpse of her oversize figure. In lighter vein, he recalled the occasion when, while she was enjoying a solitary drive, her car ran out of gasoline. A garage was nearby but she had neither money nor identification. "Telephone my brother, the President of Harvard, and he will identify me," she told the garage man. Mr. Lowell was soon on the line. "What's she doing?" he asked. "She's sitting on a stone wall smoking a cigar." "That's my sister," her brother confirmed, and Miss Lowell drove off with a full tank.

Another poet had just been added to the list: a young man named Archibald MacLeish, whose *New Found Land* appeared in 1930 in a handsome limited edition. (Two years later his *Conquistador*, a narrative poem on the conquest of Mexico, would win the Pulitzer Prize.)

The 1930 list also included Margaret Ayer Barnes's *Years of Grace*, winner of the Pulitzer Prize in fiction; Samuel Eliot Morison's now classic *Builders of the Bay Colony*; Worthington C. Ford's *Letters of Henry Adams*; Harold Nicolson's *Portrait of a Diplomatist* — along with books by John Jay Chapman, Gamaliel Bradford, Rafael Sabatini, Anne Douglas Sedgwick, and Mary Austin. Recently published and still going strong were Oliver La Farge's *Laughing Boy* (another Pulitzer Prize winner); Professor George Herbert Palmer's translation of the *Odyssey*, illustrated by N. C. Wyeth; Havelock Ellis's *Man and Woman*; Claude G. Bowers's dramatic history of the post–Civil War years, *The Tragic Era*. An impressive gathering. Depression or no, 1930 must have been a banner year for Houghton Mifflin.

2

Training Program

The treasurer's comment about "young puppies" was accurate, if not wholly ingratiating. The $15 I received, in cash, every week was nice to have, but actually I should have been paying the company. In those days, HMCo had a training program for their puppies; "on-the-job training" I suppose it would be called today. Beginning in the editorial department — where I was to end up eventually — I read manuscripts till my eyes ached. Hoping to find something publishable, I was probably overgenerous, and frequently my recommendations were reversed by higher authority. (Unpublished writers who think that their manuscripts don't get read forget that there are always young editors dying to make a "discovery.") After some months of this I was moved around briefly to the art department, where I designed my first and only jacket: for Mark Howe's biography of the great mugwump, Moorfield

Storey. I put a few lines around the title and author; later someone arranged them more harmoniously. Next stop: the advertising department. My only memory of this brief tenure is of losing a "cut" (block of printing) that was overdue and desperately needed. From advertising I went quite soon to the publicity department. Here one could hardly go wrong, since the work consisted in concocting innocuous news releases about forthcoming books. The more glamorous role of entertaining famous authors was not assigned to trainees.

Next came a stint in the sales department. This involved moving to the New York office, where there were a lot of small bookstores hardly worth visiting, and where the most inept trainee could do little damage. However, my introduction to selling, as I look back on it, amounted to cruel and unnatural punishment — not intentional, I'm sure, but rather owing to the head salesman's boredom with the whole business: "What'll we do with this guy?" What he did was to send me around to a handful of third-rate accounts, some of which were seldom called upon by the publisher's representative because they didn't pay their bills. I can't recall the names of any of these stores, but the title and appearance of the book for which I was supposed to take advance orders is as firmly etched on my memory as was Calais on the heart of Mary Tudor. It was entitled *Post-War Pirate*. The author was an Englishman named Stephen King-Hall. (Some editor, his judgment deteriorating in direct ratio to distance from Boston, had doubtless been conned into purchasing

American publishing rights on a scouting trip to London.) The jacket picture, in shades of dirty gray and blue, consisted of a submarine surfacing, with a uniformed figure emerging from the hatch. When I handed this object to the bookseller with an ingratiating smile, anticipating his order, he received it gingerly, as if he preferred to use forceps. Then came the dénouement. This was not an "advance copy." The book had been published two weeks earlier, orders had already been taken (or, more accurately, not taken), so what was I doing here anyway?

The longest and by far the best part of the training program took place in none of the publishing departments. The venerable Riverside Press, located in Cambridge on the bank of the Charles, had been one with Houghton Mifflin from the start. It was famous nationwide for the quality of its work — such as the Riverside Classics in the schools, and in the "trade," for books whose design and printing carried on the tradition of men like Berkeley Updike and Bruce Rogers. I doubt that I realized how lucky I was to be allowed to enter these august precincts and get in people's way while they explained to me what they were doing. The idea was that an editor should have some feeling for the physical product he is dealing with. To watch a book being made gives a sense of reality to the whole business.

At Riverside I made a halting progress through each avatar, from hot type to bound book. Authors who find

excessive the period of gestation from a manuscript to a
bound book should spend a day in a printing plant and
forever after hold their peace. Or should have then; all
this is half a century out of date. Instead of electronic
typesetters, there were monotype machines and molten
lead; instead of photographic film for offset printing
there were heavy metal plates. A couple of ancient flat-
bed (as opposed to rotary) presses were still used for
small jobs. "Folding and gathering" was supervised by
girls along an assembly line. They and the many other
attractive young women who worked at Riverside were
immortalized, long before my time, in the following
verses published by the *Harvard Lampoon*:

> Each morn she goes trippingly by
>   To her work in the Riverside Press,
> There's a right merry look in her eye
>   And a businesslike hang to her dress.
>
> She's rather too bold than too shy,
>   But that adds to her charm, I confess,
> And flirt, — well they're all pretty fly
>   That work in the Riverside Press.
>
> Great poets and novelists high,
>   Just think how your hopes of success
> Depend on the hand and the eye
>   Of the girl in the Riverside Press.

Illustrations on shiny paper were glued in place by an
elderly lady wielding an instrument somewhere between a ruler and a meat-chopper, with which she deftly

opened the unbound sheets where each picture was to go. Special books might be printed on rag paper, and occasionally there would be a leather binding job, perhaps with gilt edges. A fatherly character took time off to show me how it was done. After sizing the edges of the bound sheets, he would lift up a tiny sheet of gold leaf with a sort of miniature spatula and gently blow it onto the surface, rubbing it smooth with something like a rubber eraser, which was later melted down to recycle the surplus gold.

Before I leave the Riverside Press, allow me to rhapsodize for a moment about the almost sensuous pleasure of setting type by hand. First one learns the "case": a shallow wooden tray about two feet by three, divided into compartments, the largest and handiest for the letters most often used, beginning with *e*. Other compartments for spaces (1-m, 2-m, 3-m), punctuation marks, and so on. No labels; all to be memorized. In the left hand one holds the "stick," adjusted to the desired length of line. The type goes in upside down, each word followed by a "3-m" space. When the line is full, thicker spaces are inserted to make a tight fit; this is known as justifying the line. It is the tricky part: deciding what looks right to the eye, where to split a word, and so on. (In his course on the history of the printed book, Professor George Parker Winship of Harvard used to tell of an old typesetter whose uncanny skill was a mystery — until someone observed that he chewed tobacco while at work, squirting a thin stream of juice to hold the type in place as he justified the line.

He also, when setting a volume of verse, would occasionally change a word to make the line look better. "Always improved the poetry," he said.)

The stick full, it is read for errors — reading, of course, upside down and from right to left (a skill surprisingly easy to acquire, but rarely found today). The whole page is then removed and locked up in a frame (or "chase"), from which the mold for the metal plate will be made.

During my schooling at Riverside I acquired from a friend's cellar a small press powered by a pedal. This was useful to play with for bits of "job printing" from type: Christmas cards, menus for *Lampoon* dinners, invitations for cocktail parties set in the form of a cocktail glass, and like frivolities. I never had to buy type; the compositors at the press allowed me to help myself from the "hell box," where type from the monotype machines was dumped after printing, to be melted down and reused. Except for one sourpuss who specialized in setting title pages, the compositors seemed to be a contented lot. Thanks in large measure, I imagine, to the personality of Riverside's (and later Houghton Mifflin's) president, Henry A. Laughlin, the whole place had a sort of family feeling about it. Old-fashioned paternalism, no doubt. But very effective. And as preparation for a job dealing with ideas and abstractions, I found that an acquaintance with type-metal had its points.

3
The
Park Street
Office

Two PARK STREET was not, alas, designed by Charles Bulfinch, like the State House and the row of elegant private houses, beginning with the George Ticknor mansion, that once stretched down from Beacon Street to "Brimstone Corner." (A photograph of how the street looked in the mid-nineteenth century hung in the front hall of the Houghton Mifflin office.) But neither is it the standard modern office building: one of those high-rise human termitiaries with cell-blocks sealed against fresh air. Tall windows invite the winter sun — and the summer heat. No two offices are alike. Before HMCo took over, this had been a Christian Science Reading Room. And sometime in the past, according to an early janitor, it had been a goldsmith's shop, which led to the conjecture that gold dust could still be found in the cracks between the floor boards.

When all the other divisions of the company moved together to One Beacon Street, the Trade Division, to the surprise of the management, dug in its heels and stayed put — a decision eloquently supported by our leading authors. They felt at home here. Where else would one rise to one's destination in an ancient "cage" elevator, whose charming operator, Annie Williams, kept a vase of fresh flowers hanging from the grillwork and gave the visitors a welcome that no professional receptionist could hope to match?

The reception room on the second floor matured in grace and comfort over the years. Here in the corner stood the telephone switchboard, presided over by a series of genial and efficient young ladies. Much has been lost with the coming of direct dialing. For some years we had an operator whose warm and musical voice made "Good *morn*-ing, Houghton *Miff*-lin" into a song of welcome. Another, who read our books and was familiar with many of the writers, would occasionally add her own touch when I made a long-distance call. She would warm up the author, so to speak, with a bit of friendly chitchat before turning the line over to me. Talk about public relations!

Opposite the switchboard lay Two Park Street's one and only elegant chamber, in my time the directors' room, its tall windows looking out on Boston Common, its walls covered with that classic (if confused) French wallpaper depicting the early American scene, peopled by black Indians in turbans (Jackie Kennedy later installed the same paper in the downstairs entrance to the White House). In one corner stood the desk used by Nathaniel Hawthorne, one of the notable ancestors of our publishing operation. Before the company "went public," annual stockholders' meetings were held here. During Henry Laughlin's presidency they were like family gatherings: always on the mantelpiece, a flower arrangement by his wife, Becky, Henry presiding with a warmth and light touch that enlivened the cold figures and the routine votes. He enjoyed every minute of it, and his pleasure was contagious.

At the opposite corner from the directors' room, close by the venerable gravestones of the Granary Burying Ground, one found the modest office where — strained at times but never missing a beat — dwelt the financial heart of the whole operation. Every morning at precisely nine o'clock James Duncan Phillips stepped briskly from the elevator (he had once been a champion walker) and made a sharp left turn, the tails of his overcoat swirling about him as he hastened to his beloved balance sheets. Of his forceful and efficient guidance of the company's affairs others can speak more knowingly than I, since his interests were more in the educational than in the Trade Department. For example, he once remarked to me that he saw no reason why we should deal with literary agents. Theoretically, he had a point. As Ferris Greenslet — with his penchant for biological metaphor — used to say, "When three sleep in a bed, one sleeps in the middle." But the fact is that at least half the writers on our list were handled by agents, and they were growing more influential every year. Eventually, however, Duncan Phillips himself, without benefit of an agent, became one of our authors with his scholarly histories of Salem in the seventeenth and eighteenth centuries. Which reminds me of the ceremony at Salem's Essex Institute when Esther Forbes, in honor of her novel *The Running of the Tide*, was presented with the keys of the city. Duncan Phillips, scheduled to be the principal speaker, was ill; his brother Steven took his place. Steve was a man of few words. He began by saying that he didn't read novels, implying that they were a waste of time. But the night before, in preparation for this occasion, he had read the opening chapters of Esther's book. There was a note of mild surprise in his voice as he delivered the ultimate accolade: "I believe," he said, "I do believe that I may finish it!"

Though I cannot recall any editor using a quill pen or blotting his letters with sand, some office procedures in those days would have appalled a modern efficiency expert. Take, for example, the method of recording "corrigenda," i.e., the corrections to be made in the next printing of a book. In an operation that must have antedated the invention of the typewriter and carbon paper, sharp-eyed Mr. Allen would fill out a "corrigenda slip"; and while the ink was still wet he would apply this slip to a page in a bound volume of absorbent tissue. In short, an old-fashioned letter book. Fortunately, the efficient proofreaders at the Riverside Press kept errors to a minimum. Yet on at least one occasion they were overzealous. An anthology of comic short stories contained "The Treasurer's Report" by Robert Benchley: a humorous tale about the bumbling treasurer of a social organization, unaccustomed to handling figures, who gets himself and his report into an increasingly hopeless muddle. When the book was already bound, it appeared that the proofreader at Riverside had conscientiously corrected all the arithmetic.

One of the venerable institutions at Park Street was an imposing, sharp-tongued lady in black named Miss Plunkett. All matters concerned with the Riverside Press — and a good deal else — went over her desk, which to modern eyes would look like a pile of papers assembled for recycling. Yet her retrieval capacity matched that of today's computers. She was patient with ignorant neophytes. The one thing that annoyed her was to be chivvied by an editor eagerly awaiting a new book from the Press: "Am I the god that governs the drying of ink?"

Above the second floor, Two Park Street was Trade Department turf. Power was divided between Roger Scaife, general manager, and Ferris Greenslet, the editorial director — i.e., editor-in-chief — who summoned his subordinates not with electric buzzers but with a few bars on his flute. (Some years later, Mr. Scaife left

Houghton Mifflin for Little, Brown, and subsequently became head of Harvard University Press. And by the time I took over from Mr. Greenslet as editorial director, the management of the Trade Department had come into the competent hands of Lovell Thompson. For a quarter of a century he was a leading figure in shaping the character of our enterprise. Concerned more with good books than with quick and easy profits, he proved that excellence can indeed be profitable.)

On my first day at Park Street, Mr. Greenslet presented me with a copy of Sir Stanley Unwin's *The Truth About Publishing* that, from his own publishing experience, he had annotated for the American market. In the opinion of the editor of the *Saturday Review of Literature*, Greenslet was one of the last of the "literary" publishers. He had made a name for himself as a literary critic in New York before coming to work under Bliss Perry on the *Atlantic Monthly*, then owned by Houghton Mifflin. (Contrary to common assumption, Boston publishing has not been dominated by Bostonians. Henry Laughlin came from Pittsburgh, Ferris Greenslet from upstate New York. The famous *Atlantic* editor, William Dean Howells, came here from Ohio. In my time the magazine was run by editors from New Jersey and Nebraska. The president of Little, Brown was a New Yorker. And so it went.)

"F.G.," as he liked to be known, set the tone of the editorial department. I'll not try to speak for him; he told his own story, over forty years ago, in his erudite and evocative autobiography, *Under the Bridge*. I'm glad to say, however, that I had some influence on the way he told it. The original version was written in the third person, like *The Education of Henry Adams*. His intention may have been to appear modest. The effect was the opposite. He saw the point, and shifted to the conventional first person.

As his title suggests, fishing for trout was almost as important to him as fishing for authors. The two occupations, he felt, had much in common. A chapter of his autobiography is devoted to one of his greatest publishing triumphs: the acquisition of *The Education*. "From many a river," he writes, "I had learned that the way to capture a wise old reluctant trout is to keep after him; to compel him to rise, if not from appetite, perhaps at last, from irritation." Henry Adams, to judge from his own correspondence, was not difficult to irritate.

Greenslet had contributed a chapter to a lavish volume entitled *The Book of the Fly Rod*, printed in England and published the year I came to Park Street. A split-bamboo rod in its aluminum case rested in one corner of his office; on the wall was a framed poem on fly fishing written for him by John Buchan, Lord Tweedsmuir.

F.G.'s favorite form of discourse was the anecdote. His store was bottomless, his verbal memory astonishing. Always the exact quotation, always the *mot juste*. I recall one occasion when we were in the office elevator together. I had made some remark that he apparently thought clever, and so assumed that it was a quotation. "Where did you get that?" he asked. If I'd been on my toes I would have answered: "Somewhere between the first and the second floor."

His special sense of humor is, for me, immortalized in a personal anecdote about fly fishing. Having parked his car one summer morning beside a favorite New Hampshire stream, he noticed a motorcycle with sidecar and creel already standing there. The water was low and the fishing poor, but he did manage to take two plump, ten-inch trout. He never encountered the other fishermen, but before leaving he took a peek into their creel. There lay two small, skinny, barely legal-size trout. More interested in catching fish than in eating them, he tossed these pitiful objects into the bushes, substituted his own catch exactly where they had lain, and drove off. I still delight in the thought of those two fishermen when they returned from the river and opened their creel.

Greenslet liked to say that the ideal publishing house would consist of an editor and his secretary. His method of choosing a "dactylograph" — to use his favorite term — began by inviting the young lady to sit down and take off her hat. This now outdated ploy was doubtless intended to test the applicant's poise. Perhaps it was also a screen for his own shyness. In any case, he chose well, though none could spell the Latin tags with which he ornamented his correspondence. Unwilling to admit her ignorance, his secretary would come to my office next door for help. Between us we could generally save her the embarrassment of going back to him.

To keep up with the flow of manuscripts was an ever-lasting struggle. No editor could be expected to read them all. F.G., however, was adept at quick sampling. In his own words: "If you prick it, does it bleed?" As any chief editor must, he would approve a manuscript not to his personal taste if he had confidence in the editor recommending it. Yet he had a favorite slogan: "When in doubt, decline." This seems to me a questionable rule, if taken literally. I should put it somewhat differently. When later I had such decisions to make, I was inclined to take the risk on a manuscript that, shall we say, two readers disliked and two others fiercely championed. Another offering, though all the reports were mildly favorable, might safely be declined.

(Alfred McIntyre, the wise and sensitive president of Little, Brown, reputedly had his own personal procedure when occasionally called upon to judge a novel. He would take the manuscript home, and after dinner sit down in comfort with a scotch and soda. If, after a second highball, it brought tears to his eyes, he would recommend publication.)

In his autobiography F.G. described himself as "fifty percent executive and factual, the other moiety literary and fanciful." Offhand, this sounds like the perfect formula for an editor. So it was — and is. But the price, he recalled, was "a civil war in my innards." In his case, the source of peace and renewal was to be found in the gin-clear waters of a trout stream.

4
Writer and Editor

WHEN I RETURNED to Park Street from the training program at the Riverside Press, one of my jobs was to greet strangers who turned up unannounced, wanting to see the editor. Generally I managed to keep them happy, but there were notable failures. Witness the dreamy, unworldly woman who appeared with a sheaf of poems "that Shelley and I have written together." When I said that we should be glad to consider them, she would have none of it. She wanted a contract, then and there. At last, sadly, she took them back. Her disappointment was mingled with scorn as she departed. "I thought," she declared with slow solemnity, "I thought . . . I'd see . . . a *white-haired* man." I had failed her. I could do better now.

A young editor was also a convenient repository for manuscripts of dubious literary worth that had been

accepted for publication for some special reason, such as
the insistence of a salesman who promised a good sale
in his territory. One morning Mr. Greenslet appeared
with a look of distaste and slapped down a well-stuffed
envelope on my desk as if it were a catfish that had
inadvertently swallowed his trout-fly. "Here!" he
growled. "Take the goose grease out of this." The title
of the manuscript was *Health, Beauty and Charm* —
written by a Hollywood beautician and forcefully
recommended by our West Coast salesman, Harrison
Leussler, familiarly known as The Sheriff. Had I followed instructions literally, there would have been little
left to publish. But I'm sure the book had a fine sale —
at least on the West Coast. My certainty is based on a
day spent with The Sheriff as he made his rounds of
the Los Angeles bookstores. Tall, heavy-featured, loudly
genial, and wearing a ten-gallon hat, he had earned his
sobriquet. He didn't ask the buyers how many copies
of each title they wanted. He told them. His cordial
slap on the back had left them breathless anyway. And
who were they to defy the law?

Another editorial assignment, in 1933, was more fun
and more fruitful. Over half a century later, it is still a
pleasure to recollect. Our managing editor in those days,
Ira Rich Kent, had just returned from Washington,
where he had succeeded in obtaining the book publishing rights of a unique mass of material: the reminiscences of the late Irwin Hood (Ike) Hoover. Hoover

had come to the White House in 1891 as a young employee of the Edison Company to install the first electric lights during the presidency of Benjamin Harrison. He had planned to leave when the job was done. But "the Harrison family were actually afraid to turn the lights on and off for fear of getting a shock." So he stayed to handle the switches and eventually to become chief usher of the White House, on intimate terms with ten Presidents and their families. He was still on hand to greet Franklin and Eleanor Roosevelt.

Ike had begun to write his reminiscences when he died in the fall of 1933. The bulk of the material remained in rough notes, scrambled in time and subject matter, ranging from amusing trivia to a unique account of Woodrow Wilson's fateful trip to Europe following World War I and the dark days that ensued when his collapse left the country without a President. Wilson Ike worshiped, Teddy Roosevelt he loved, Calvin Coolidge he could not bear.

For a young editor, making a semblance of cosmos out of this chaos was good on-the-job training. Published in 1934, *Forty-Two Years in the White House* became a best seller. For occupants of that house (those who read books) it remains a source of enjoyment and even, perhaps, of instruction.

ॐ

An essential part of an editor's job is of course the uncovering of new talent. A useful tool for that purpose has been the Houghton Mifflin Literary Fellowships.

Established in 1935, they have served their purpose for more than half a century. That purpose is to help young writers, hitherto unpublished in book form, to complete their first book projects. Credit for the original idea belongs to Lovell Thompson, later to become manager of the Trade Department. The plan was somewhat similar to that of the Guggenheim fellowships but, so far as I know, the first of its sort in commercial publishing. The initial response was encouraging, and the early Fellowship winners set a high standard. (The standard would have been even higher if we had been shrewd enough to recognize all the talent that appeared in embryo.)

The author of our first Fellowship book was E. P. (Pat) O'Donnell: a dark peppery little man with a warm — almost sentimental — streak. He had done jobs of all sorts; most recently he had been a cook on a transatlantic freighter and a worker in the Ford assembly plant in New Orleans. There he met Sherwood Anderson — who must have been touring the plant — and apparently Anderson had read a story of his, in *Story* magazine perhaps, and encouraged him to keep on. When I first heard from Pat he was living in the Mississippi Delta. He submitted a sample manuscript with a horrible title: "Spume on the Pollen," which sounds like someone spitting but was in fact a reference to a scene in the projected novel where a Cajun is illegally growing Easter lilies on someone else's land beside the ocean.

When the complete manuscript came in, Ferris Greenslet and I struggled over a title, armed with Bartlett's *Familiar Quotations*. We came across a phrase in Milton, "margents green." It occurred to me that below New Orleans the strange Delta country shores — which in places are literally afloat — are technically known as margins. So we modified Milton and turned him upside down and came out with *Green Margins*. To everyone's surprise — since the judges rarely chose first novels — *Green Margins* was taken by the Book-of-the-Month Club.

At about this time I visited Pat in the little shack where he lived, seventy-five miles south of New Orleans in the Delta, a land formed by silt, wholly without rocks. (Once, Pat told me, he had brought back a small rock in his car from a trip north. To the Delta people it was a wonder; they handed it around from one to another, as they fondled it and marveled at it, until, when they returned it to him, it was warm from their bodies.) The trip down from New Orleans was largely through citrus groves, growing right up to the edge of the high levees. When we eventually reached Pat's shack, we had supper consisting of a pail of fresh shrimp. Before falling asleep I felt, rather than heard, a deep rhythmic beat, a gentle heaving of the earth below us as the huge propeller of a freighter turned slowly on its way upstream.

Later visits were in New Orleans, since Pat had moved back to the city, living in "Pirates Alley," a

narrow cobbled street bordering the cathedral, where
he shared a flat with two flying squirrels. Here I met his
girl, Mary King, who had recently published a fine
short story in the *Yale Review* — at that time one of the
best outlets for new writers. In due course she also
became a Fellowship author and her second book a
choice of the Literary Guild.

Another Literary Fellowship winner, Jennie Ballou,
was 100 percent the opposite of Mary. Jennie could be
difficult. On one visit to Park Street she argued with me
vehemently over something or other that we had agreed
upon. When I produced correspondence to prove my
point, she was not convinced, only more angry than
ever. "You're the kind of man," she spat, "who keeps
carbon copies!" But there was a good deal of talent
underlying all this nonsense. Her Fellowship novel
about prerevolutionary Spain, *Spanish Prelude*, was
called by one reviewer "so original and so curiously
fascinating that it is hard to communicate one's own
sense of excitement" — the sort of writing that the
Literary Fellowships were designed to uncover.

Those early Fellowship books included one "modern
classic," Dorothy Baker's *Young Man with a Horn*, a
novel based on the career of Bix Beiderbecke, the great
jazz musician. Her application was accompanied by
some sixty pages of sample manuscript, which, though
later discarded, were enough to show her talent. Her
project was wholly original: "a new voice in the wilderness," as Emerson might have put it. Later books were

less successful. As is too often the case with novelists, it is her first book by which she is remembered. This is probably true also of Carson McCullers, author of *The Heart Is a Lonely Hunter* who, though not a Fellowship winner, received her first contract under the plan.

Such were the beginnings of the Fellowship idea. It worked so well from the start that it soon received the compliment of imitation, when a New York publisher announced a competing fellowship. In doing so he copied our brochure word for word, changing only "Houghton Mifflin will expect to publish . . ." to "I shall expect to cause publication of . . ." and upping the ante by $200. But he soon gave it up.

Today the list of writers whose first books were helped along by these Fellowships is a long one, with a fair number of familiar names, including Robert Penn Warren, Elizabeth Bishop, Arthur Mizener, Charles Bracelen Flood, Edward Hoagland, Philip Roth. Many of those selected continued to write for Houghton Mifflin; others, once launched, sought their future elsewhere. But in a modest way, the plan has made its contribution to the publishing scene.

F.G.'s comments on the schizophrenic nature of a book editor's job brings to mind a penetrating article by Jack Fischer, former editor of *Harper's Magazine*, in which he dwelt on a perhaps less obvious conflict. The more sensitive the editor, the more difficult it is for him to turn down a manuscript on which a writer has pinned his hopes and his self-esteem. If, in self-protection, the editor trains himself to remain detached, emotionally uninvolved, he becomes that much less good at his job. Of course, he can seek refuge in the thought that, with the proliferation of publishers and the competition for manuscripts, few worth publishing fail eventually to find a home. An easy and not quite honest way out.

One fact I learned fairly early: the value to an editor of having some professional experience as a writer. One can accept, intellectually, the cliché that an author's book is his brainchild, almost as precious as the child of his loins. But it takes rare powers of projection to appreciate what this means. For most of us, it is a salutary exercise occasionally to leap the fence, to see how things appear from the other side — as I did from time to time by writing magazine articles, principally for the *Atlantic*.

There existed at Park Street during my time a strong sense of continuity on both sides of the fence. Most of the executives had started out early with the company and stayed on to run it. Most of the authors, once on the list, were inclined to stay there. "Shopping around" was less in fashion. And though readers seldom notice publishers' imprints, the writer who kept changing from house to house did not enhance his reputation with the book trade.

One can argue that this feeling of loyalty to a publisher, and the corresponding sense of obligation on the latter's part, is sentimental nonsense. Why not auction off each book for what it will fetch? A simple answer is that the early books of many best-selling authors would not have fetched anything. More fundamentally, we are dealing here with the unique character of the publishing business. As I once wrote in a lighthearted article for the *Atlantic* on the nature of book contracts:

A book contract is the record of an act of faith. It is necessarily so from both the author's and the publisher's point of view. The author is committing his dearest possession, his most cherished offspring, to other hands. His attitude henceforth must be not that of the mammal which suckles its young, but that of the tortoise which lays its eggs in the sand and leaves them to be hatched by the heat of the sun. The publisher is also acting on faith: faith in the salability of the book, faith in the author's future, faith — in many instances — that the book will be written.

Such a contract, despite its legal trappings and businesslike appearance, is not like a will or a deed or a commercial agreement under which certain things will inevitably happen or the parties will be brought to court. It involves a continuously creative process with all the uncertainty and risk that implies. It can never guarantee results.

It can, however, serve as a memorandum of obligations and intentions, between two parties with a common objective. The author-publisher (particularly the author-editor) relationship is a professional one, at least in the dictionary sense of "not purely commercial." It is not purely anything. It is compounded of friendship, sympathy, exasperation, patience, understanding, mis-understanding, hand-holding, prodding, rapiers, brick-bats, and a solid front against the rest of the world. In short, it is based, like all sound professional relation-ships, on mutual confidence. A good publisher does not try to hold an author by legal means any more than a good doctor tries to hold a patient who is convinced that he can get better treatment somewhere else. When con-fidence is lacking on either side, there is every reason for a new deal.

Yet on occasion the reason is so trivial as to seem absurd. Witness the break with Willa Cather — a tragic event for Houghton Mifflin that had occurred before my time but was still the subject of speculation. Greenslet had "discovered" her, understood and en-couraged her, published her first four novels. A framed photograph and a letter from her hung beside John Buchan on his office wall. What had happened? Some said that she had quarreled with Roger Scaife over a jacket, or advertising. The true story was later told to me by Alfred Knopf, to whom she had gone after leaving Park Street. She explained to him that Mr. Greenslet had taken the liberty of addressing her in a letter as "Dear Willa." Such familiarity she apparently found offensive, though they had known each other for years. So she left. Hard to believe, but Alfred had it straight from her.

Sauce for the goose — the respect that Miss Cather considered her due — can be poison for the gander. Many years later, Thomas Wolfe left Scribners and was looking for a new publisher. I met him in our New York office, was subjected to a torrent of Wolfian prose as he strode about the room, discarding his jacket and loosening his tie, like an actor playing Wolfe to a one-man audience. I concluded Act One by inviting him to bring over his manuscripts, which were (almost too pat to believe) in Brooklyn's "Mammoth Warehouse." Next morning there was barely room to enter the little office reserved for editors from Boston. A trunk-size wooden packing case stood on the floor, eight cartons covered desk and chairs. Sampling the contents of the packing case disclosed layers of typescript between layers of dirty shirts. The cartons contained copy mixed with domestic litter; one held nothing but rolls of toilet paper. This, however, is as far as my investigation went.

Bob Linscott, one of our shrewdest editors, was also in New York. He had spent a happy and bibulous evening with Tom, and wrote to him immediately on returning to Boston. But he made a fatal mistake. Elizabeth Nowell, Wolfe's agent and biographer, describes the incident.

What upset him [Tom] . . . was that the letter addressed him as "Dear Wolfe" although Linscott had asked

permission to call him Tom and had done so with great
warmth and cordiality. As Wolfe said later, in a fictional
account of this experience, which described it as having
happened to a writer named Jim Smith: ". . . The
author cannot help remembering that the publisher
asked if he could call him Jim when they were having
drinks together over the dinner table, but calls him
Smith when he writes a business letter . . . The publisher
did not tell him that it was going to be Jim in friendship
and in editing, but Smith in business. He led the author
to believe, with his talk of faith and belief and support
and the privilege and the honor of publishing the
author, that it was going to be Jim all the time . . . But
when Jim finds out that it is always Smith when a
question of business advantage, of profit or loss, is
concerned . . . then there is likely to be trouble."

Thomas Wolfe found offensive what Willa Cather
demanded. He went elsewhere.

ॐ

We had been more successful in taking on a then-
unknown writer, James Agee. Since his death in 1955
so much has been written about Agee's life and work —
including an exhaustive biography — that I shall con-
fine myself to a brief account of the publication of his
first great book, *Let Us Now Praise Famous Men*.

At Harvard, where he was a year behind me (he was
class of 1932), I had of course been aware of him as a
poet and the distinguished president of the *Harvard*

Advocate, but that was about all. In the spring of his senior year, the *Advocate* published, with a good deal of fanfare, a parody of *Time* magazine, which had the result — not wholly unanticipated — of getting him a job: first on *Time*, later on *Fortune*.

Jim was not the sort of writer one would expect to find in the Luce empire. What, I wonder, did the editors of *Fortune* expect when they commissioned him and Walker Evans to do a documentary story on the Alabama sharecroppers? Walker had already made a reputation with his photographs of rural America, commissioned during the Depression by the Farm Security Administration. Neither he nor Jim — least of all the latter — would seem likely choices for such an assignment. Here is the opening statement, later written by Agee, master of the nonstop sentence:

It seems to me curious, not to say obscene and thoroughly terrifying, that it could occur to an association of human beings drawn together through need and chance and for profit into a company, an organ of journalism, to pry intimately into the lives of an undefended and appallingly damaged group of human beings, an ignorant and helpless rural family, for the purpose of parading the nakedness, disadvantage and humiliation of these lives before another group of human beings, in the name of science, of "honest journalism" (whatever that paradox may mean), of humanity, of social fearlessness, for money, and for a reputation for crusading and for unbias which, when skillfully enough qualified, is exchangeable at any bank for money (and in politics, for votes, job patronage, abelincolnism, etc.); and that these people could be capable of meditating this prospect without the slightest doubt of their qualification to do an "honest" piece of work, and with a conscience better than clear, and in the virtual certitude of almost unanimous public approval. It seems curious, further, that the assignment of this work should have fallen to persons having so extremely different a form of respect for the subject, and responsibility toward it...

Not surprisingly, the *Fortune* editors turned the piece down, and Jim and Walker were free to find a book publisher if they could. Harper's contracted to publish *Let Us Now Praise Famous Men*, but there was one hitch: those "four-letter words." In discussing the problem with Jim, his editor at Harper's unfortunately showed Jim a memorandum from the senior editor, which said in effect that he himself didn't mind these words, but he feared they would offend his readers. Agee, furious, said that he would publish with Harper's on one condition, i.e., that they publish that (here, presumably, followed all the four-letter words in adjectival form) memorandum of their senior editor in the front of the book. Relations became strained. Meanwhile Walker Evans, in checking the proofs of his photographs, had noticed to his dismay that the engraver had cleaned up the picture of the white counterpane on the sharecropper's bed by removing the fly

specks. Such tampering was heresy. What with one
thing and another, the Harper's contract was canceled.
(Before printing the photographs, HMCo had the flyspecks restored. Under a magnifying glass, one can see
that they were made by an engraver's tool.)

Fortunately I got wind of the situation from Eunice
Clark Jessup (whose husband was chief editorial writer
for *Life*), Jim's friend and a literary scout for HMCo.
Jim sent us the manuscript — which had been lying
dormant since the Harper's blowup, though perhaps
one other publisher had seen it. Reports were enthusiastic, the Executive Committee voted to publish (the
treasurer, I understand, thought from the title that it
was a book about famous characters in history), and all
was well, with the exception of those four-letter words.
I called Walker — a calm and reasonable man except
when people tamper with flyspecks — and told him
that we were making no judgments on propriety or
good taste or what have you, and that we intended to
make only such deletions as were necessary to allow the
book to be printed and sold under Massachusetts law.
He agreed that this made sense, and persuaded Jim to
go along.

I went to New York City with a contract for them
to sign — principally to see Jim, who had certain publication problems on his mind. "Just one small point,"
he said, gesturing with his strong, beautiful hands as
if he were picking a scrap of paper out of the air.
"Would it not be better if Houghton Mifflin, instead of

paying me a royalty, put me on a permanent salary?" I
suggested that this was somewhat premature; shouldn't
we wait for his second book? He consented. He had
two other requests: that the book be printed on the
cheapest possible paper such as newsprint, and that it
have a plain jacket. I pointed out that such paper would
turn to powder in a few years. Might be a good thing,
he replied, but he didn't insist. As for the jacket, I
agreed. (I think that both he and Walker liked the
jacket: bold white lettering against the dark red earth
of a plowed field.)

With World War II looming on the horizon, 1941
was not an auspicious year for publication. *Let Us Now
Praise Famous Men* at first received some perceptive
but many devastating reviews; it sold about 600 copies.
Only later was its quality recognized. Republished post-
humously in 1960, it sold very well indeed, and was
selected by the Book Find Club. (There is a close par-
allel with Rachel Carson. Her first book, published just
before Pearl Harbor, was hardly noticed outside professional circles. When reissued following *The Sea Around
Us*, it went right onto the best-seller list.)

Let Us Now Praise Famous Men has been described
as a "classic work of dissent," comparable to the writings of Henry D. Thoreau. One is reminded of
Thoreau's remark: "I desire to speak somewhere without bounds . . . for I am convinced that I cannot
exaggerate enough even to lay the foundation of a true

expression." As with Thoreau, full appreciation of Agee's work may come long after his death. Both writers died all too soon — in their midforties.

No matter how many writers an editor may have worked with, there is almost always some special quality, or some memorable moment that evokes a vivid recollection of each. Take for example Esther Forbes, who was already on the Houghton Mifflin list when I arrived, and quite soon became a close friend. Her knowledge of early New England was staggering, her historical novels were magic re-creations of the past. Her Pulitzer Prize winning biography of Paul Revere, as well as its offshoot, *Johnny Tremain*, are modern classics. In her writing she was above all a craftsman, skillful and, when necessary, ruthless in shaping her own work. When for instance she agreed with me that the opening chapter of one of her novels was an un-needed encumbrance, she promptly threw it out, with no apparent regrets for the time she had spent on it. It had served its purpose in getting her started. And speaking of getting started, Esther once discovered a surprising cure for "writer's block." Before my time, she had worked as an editorial reader at Park Street; when we were shorthanded during my stint in London for the Office of War Information, she returned to her old job three days a week. This limit on her time for creative writing somehow started up the engine. In the remaining four days she was soon producing more copy than she previously had done in seven.

Never have I known a major writer with more modesty: if she ever boasted, it was not about her books but about her experience driving a team of farm horses in the Women's Land Army during the First World War. Yet she always held firmly to her literary convictions. A case in point is *Johnny Tremain*, her story for young readers. Owing to a temporary misunderstanding with Ferris Greenslet, she offered the manuscript to a New York publisher. They accepted it, with the proviso that she "vocabularize" the language to make it easier reading for a certain age group, on the assumption that children did not want to be faced with unfamiliar words. Bring it to Park Street, we told her, and we'll print it exactly as it stands. Children *like* to learn new words. The judges for the Newbery Medal — the top award for children's literature — apparently agreed.

Unlike Esther Forbes, Anya Seton (daughter of the famous nature writer and artist, Ernest Thompson Seton) had certain qualities of the prima donna, fortunately tempered by a warm personality and a sense of humor. She will not, like some of the writers I have mentioned, be remembered for her first book. Her best work came later. Unluckily her early romantic novels resulted in her being "typed" by some reviewers as a popular writer not to be taken seriously. In fact her major historical fiction was based on intense research, concealed perhaps by her skill in telling a dramatic story. Before putting pen to paper she plumbed the archives and quite literally covered the ground where the action takes place. While working on *Katherine*, her novel about the colorful ancestor of five monarchs of England, she spent months familiarizing herself with the countryside and retracing the journeys of her protagonist. If she wrote about Katherine's equipage getting stuck in the spring mud, she had learned from observation on the spot that this was a likely event.

Anya's later novels — *Katherine, The Winthrop Woman* — won for her a wide audience both here and abroad, as well as very substantial royalties. (*Katherine* was No. 1 on the English best-seller list, No. 2 in America.) But she told me, and I believe her, that the response to her work that she treasured most was the letter she received from the leading authority in England on the Chaucerian period, the setting for *Katherine*. Her book, he told her, was the most authentic fictional representation of that era in English history that he had ever read.

Working with Anya was largely a matter of lending an appreciative, if sometimes critical, ear. Contributions from me were mostly minor, though she did once credit me with helping to round out a novel that, in first draft, had a good beginning and a good ending but no middle. These editorial sessions generally entailed an overnight visit to her home in Greenwich, Connecticut. Though always enjoyable, they invariably left me feeling like a sucked egg.

An author's most successful book, in terms of sales, is not always one's personal favorite. Ben Ames Williams was among the most productive and successful novelists on the Houghton Mifflin list. His books, like Anya's, showed a rising curve of sales. Professional and prolific, he wrote both romantic novels and serious historical fiction, the latter culminating in his *magnum opus, House Divided*, a Civil War novel of over fifteen hundred pages. Yet for me the most delightful and compelling book of all is *Come Spring*, the story of the founding of a town in the wilderness of Maine during the years of the American Revolution. Published in 1940, it was correctly presented to the book trade as "utterly different from the 'historical novels' that the American public has been reading in recent years." Ben knew every acre of the country he wrote about. When my wife and I visited him and his wife (by bicycle) at their lovely old farmhouse in Searsmont, we paddled his canoe up the nearby St. George's River, scene of the opening chapter of *Come Spring*. On the book's endpapers are printed detailed maps of the river (and of the colonial town that in 1780 became Union, Maine) indicating the location of each family in his story.

Ben Williams was an outdoor man. If you want to

know how to notch a tree to make it fall just so, to raise a barn, to hunt a bear or moose, it's all there. In this he resembled his good friend on another publisher's list, Kenneth Roberts, certain of whose novels can almost be used as guidebooks to the terrain they cover. (On a trip down Lake Champlain, as Susie and I approached Valcour Island, a copy of Roberts's *Rabble in Arms* brought to life for us a decisive battle of the American Revolution, when we compared the speed of Benedict Arnold's gunboats with that of our canoe under sail.)

Another outdoorsman on our list, David Walker — born a Scot and now a resident of Canada — wrote more in the manner of an earlier Park Street author, John Buchan. (He had served as aide-de-camp to Buchan — by then Lord Tweedsmuir — Canada's Governor General immediately before the Second World War.) His idyllic love story, *Geordie*, about a little lad in a Highland village who made himself a world-famous athlete, won him a large audience here and in Great Britain. But here again the book I recall with the greatest admiration had a more modest sale. Entitled *The Pillar*, it grew out of the author's own wartime experience: the story of six British soldiers of utterly different backgrounds thrown together in a German prison camp, their conflicts and intimacies, their daring attempts to escape, the pillar of companionship that enabled them to survive.

Just as a writer's most salable books may not necessarily be those that endure longest in one's memory, so his or her work as a whole may have a lasting impact quite independent of appearances on the best-seller lists. I think of Esther Warner (now Esther Dendel) whose artistic training and empathy with other cultures led to a number of books, beginning with *New Song in a Strange Land*, that are perhaps unique in their intimate knowledge, based on personal friendships, of the life and art of the people of West Africa. For her, as for that artist in many fields, William Morris (whose work she greatly admires), art is not something to be displayed in museums, but an essential aspect of daily living. "I wish," she says, "that the word had never been invented."

Although most of Esther's books have done well, none of them has had a sensational sale. But they will endure.

ε∾

The majority of the writers on our list came to Park Street as a result of one connection or another. James Russell Lowell, when he was editor of the prestigious *Atlantic Monthly*, is said to have boasted that he never needed to seek out writers for his magazine. They came to him. Those days are gone, for both magazine and book publishers. Unsolicited manuscripts — those that arrive unheralded in the mail ("over the transom," in publisher's jargon) — get careful reading, but few turn out to be publishable. There are, however, notable exceptions. For example, in late 1948 we received the manuscript of a novel about life in a Mormon community by someone named Ardyth Kennelly. The accompanying letter was charmingly brief. It said, in effect, that she was sending it to Houghton Mifflin because we published Winston Churchill (*The Gathering Storm* had appeared in June) and therefore must be OK. If we didn't want it, postage for its return was enclosed. We did want it. Entitled *The Peaceable Kingdom*, it was chosen by the Literary Guild and did very well indeed.

A notable biography came to Park Street through no effort of our own, but rather because the subject of the biography, Mr. Bernard Baruch, was impressed with Margaret Coit's *Calhoun*, which had won a Pulitzer Prize. He felt that she was the ideal author to write about him — with the understanding that she would have free rein and he would not read the book until it was published. All went well until the text was in galley proof. At Mr. Baruch's request, we had sent a set of galley proofs to his secretary. Suddenly, without explanation, permission was withdrawn to quote his own words in his many interviews with Miss Coit. There were plenty of them; the task of changing all of them into indirect discourse was exhausting for the author, and endangered our publication schedule. Why the sudden change of mind? I suspect that the number of quotations flattering to Mr. Baruch, all conscientiously attributed in the notes to conversations with him, may have given an unwanted impression. Meanwhile, unbeknownst to us, he had been writing an autobiography for another publisher. Both books were published on the same day. Margaret Coit's fortunately was a Book-of-the-Month Club selection.

I'll conclude this chapter on writers and editors with a dip into the world of modern science at its most arcane. Those who would malign professors like to describe them as people who spend their lives learning more and more about less and less. It might equally be said of editors that they learn less and less about more and more. Surely I should not have known the meaning of the word *cybernetics* had I not been seeking a book from the MIT professor who coined it, Norbert Wiener.

The *American Heritage Dictionary* defines *cybernetics* as "the theoretical study of control processes in electronical, mechanical, and biological systems." In short, the principle of "feedback," on which computers are based. The word is derived from the Greek for "steersman" — I suppose because in steering a boat one has to anticipate the response to the rudder. Otherwise the bow will swing back and forth, and your wake will look like an eel in agony.

Professor Wiener, like his father before him, had been a child prodigy. Decades ago he had pointed out that we were now in the Age of Communication (i.e., of electronics); the Industrial Age was already behind us. He foresaw a time when whole factories would run without human hands, directed from a distance. And so on. If he could be persuaded to put all this down on paper, in terms that the layman could understand, we would obviously have an important book.

I had heard about Wiener from my friend and Houghton Mifflin author, Elting Morison, historian at MIT. Elting is himself an authority on the history of innovation and biographer of the great naval innovator Admiral Sims. He was not sanguine about the chances of my getting a book from the distinguished professor, who had published scientific books and papers but nothing for the general public. Wiener was mercurial and unpredictable. Other trade publishers had wooed him in vain. He was touchy. The MIT office, I am told, kept a file of his resignations on one issue or another, such as inviting that "warmonger" Winston Churchill to the Mid-Century Convocation in 1949. These resignations were routinely ignored.

Despite all this, the project was worth a try. To my surprise, the professor was very much interested. He did have a message for the general public: a warning against allowing modern technology to take over our lives. The title I suggested to him was *The Human Use of Human Beings*. Finally one spring when he had retreated to his house in New Hampshire, he got to work. Soon I received the draft of the first two chapters. Chapter 1 had nothing to do with the subject we had discussed. It was devoted entirely to his childhood and to the bitter relations with his father. It was quite impossible. Chapter 2, on the other hand, was promising. He had gotten the business with his father off his chest and was well launched on the book I had hoped for.

So what to do? Fortunately his secretary, who was working with him in New Hampshire, was an old friend of mine — obviously diplomatic and well endowed with a sense of humor, or she could never have kept that job. So I put in a person-to-person call to her (telling the operator that I did *not* want to speak with Professor Wiener) and for perhaps fifteen or twenty minutes I talked to her about that dreadful first chapter and what we could do about it. Suddenly, to my horror, Wiener himself came on the line: "Wiener here! We'll scrap the book!" I urged further discussion. "No, we'll scrap it!" To which I replied that I was halfway through a long memorandum of editorial suggestions and intended to finish it and mail it to him anyway. End of conversation.

Early next morning the telephone rang in my office. New Hampshire calling: "Wiener here. Have your memorandum. Think I can do it! Think I can do it!" And he did.

Published in 1950, reprinted in paperback, *The Human Use of Human Beings* has had a long life — possibly because the validity of Professor Wiener's concern has been so amply proven.

5
A Field Guide to
Roger Tory Peterson

I HAD BEEN at Two Park Street less than two years when I met a man who has been a close friend and an enormous asset to Houghton Mifflin for more than fifty years. (On my desk as I write is a photograph of Roger Tory Peterson, adorning the cover of the company's 1984 annual report.) One summer day in 1933 there arrived in the office that I shared with Francis H. Allen the manuscript and drawings for a new type of bird guide, already seen and rejected by five other book publishers. Soon thereafter appeared the author himself. The person he came to see was of course Mr. Allen. Today when Roger is making a public speech and knows that I am in the audience, he invariably recalls that, on his first visit to Park Street, he mistook me for the office boy. A natural error. We were both in our midtwenties, he half a year older than I. Fortunately I had by then a toehold in the editorial department and so had a chance to report on his project: "I think I am in a fairly good position to look at this book from the point of view of a beginner . . . it seems to me an excellent job." I went on to say that we could count on "a moderately good steady sale."

On that morning in 1933, Francis Allen didn't need the binoculars he always kept in his roll-top desk to realize at once that he was looking at a brand-new species of guidebook. Peterson's book, he wrote in his editorial report, "is conceived on entirely new lines. The principal feature of the book is diagrammatic drawings to show the appearance of birds in the field . . . The figures on each plate are so arranged as to bring together the species that are most similar and most likely to be confused, and the diagnostic marks of the species are pointed out by arrows . . . It is a book that would appeal not only to beginners but to the more advanced ornithologists and I think will prove practically indispensable to students of birds in the field." Trusting his judgment, his colleagues agreed to publish.

The story leading up to that notable event has often been told: The seventh-grade schoolteacher in Jamestown, New York, who started a Junior Audubon Club, encouraging her pupils to copy the pictures in the leaflets and thus setting Roger off on a frenzy of bird drawing; the five years that he spent at art schools and commercial painting in New York; the invaluable experience of birding with Ludlow Griscom, dean of field ornithologists; the summers as nature counselor at Clarence E. Allen's Camp Chewonki in Maine; the four years of teaching at the Rivers School in Brookline, Massachusetts, during which time the *Field Guide* was born. The Audubon Society's Bill Vogt, his birding companion on trips to New York, had been struck by Roger's uncanny ability to identify birds in the field. Could this be somehow transferred to the printed page, so that others less gifted might share it? Thanks to his systematic mind and his artist's sense of pattern, Roger found that it could. Using a schematic approach, with text reduced to the minimum needed for recognition, he produced a quick-reference guide unlike anything seen before.

Not that there was any lack of bird books on the market. An impressive scientific literature had accumulated since Elliott Coues published his classic *Key to North American Birds* in 1872. Later Frank M. Chapman of the American Museum of Natural History, author of the famous *Handbook of Birds of Eastern North America*, pioneered in establishing communication between the professional and the public. Bookstores had been full of bird books for the layman since the turn of the century, when the Audubon Societies were born and bird watching became a popular outdoor recreation for men and women alike. (Long outdated was the comment by an early New England naturalist that the female sex "cannot without some eccentricity of conduct follow birds and quadrupeds to the woods.")

At my elbow as I write are three "landmark" volumes: (1) *Birdcraft: A Field Book of Two Hundred Song, Game, and Water Birds* by Mabel Osgood Wright (1895), with superb drawings by the young Louis Agassiz Fuertes. The cover is decorated with a pair of Ruby-throated Hummingbirds picked out in gold leaf, on the edge of a golden nest with two gold eggs. Try that on a modern bindery! (2) *Bird-Life* by Frank M. Chapman (1898), illustrated in color by Ernest Thompson Seton: a book for beginners based on Chapman's classic *Handbook*. (3) Chapman's *Color Key to North American Birds* (1903), with drawings in black and white and in color by Chester A. Reed: the most ambitious attempt at field identification without the use of a gun. Battered and re-bound, my copy is falling apart once more, though the cardinal on the cover has survived. The drawings by Reed seem stiff and lifeless, as if made from museum specimens, and the touches of color are not much help.

However, it was Reed who produced, on his own, the inexpensive and vastly popular series of nature guides that my generation — and Roger's — was brought up on. Pocket size, they were long and narrow, with text at the left and a color picture at the right-hand margin. The *Reed Bird Guide* was standard equipment for birders. But it lacked the features of the Peterson *Field Guides* that — in the words of a leading ornithologist — would make field recognition of birds, for the first time, into a science.

In the preface to the first edition of the *Field Guide*,

Roger acknowledged his debt to Ernest Thompson Seton's drawings in *Two Little Savages*, which emphasized the "patterns" of ducks seen at a distance. He tells how he and his naturalist friends sought in vain for a book that would treat *all* birds in this manner, that would pick out the "little blotches or streaks that were their labels or identification tags . . . a boiling-down or simplification of things so that any bird could be readily and surely told *from all others* at a glance or at a distance. . . Hence this handbook."

This was a new departure among bird books. Yet it is understandable that, in the depth of the Great Depression, other publishers should have hesitated to take the risk. When, bubbling with youthful enthusiasm, I told Judge Robert Walcott, the kindly but somewhat intimidating president of the Massachusetts Audubon Society, about our new acquisition, he looked down at me compassionately over his half-moon glasses. The book, he assured me, would never sell. Who would pay $2.75 when he could buy a *Reed Bird Guide* for a dollar? A year later, having forgotten this conversation, he asked me whether I had seen the new bird guide that every ornithologist had in his pocket . . .

The first printing of the *Field Guide* was only two thousand copies. On June 10, 1934, Roger wrote exultantly to Lewis Gannett, the nature-loving reviewer for the *New York Herald Tribune:* "My *Field Guide to the Birds* is now in its second printing. The first was exhausted in a little over three weeks, due, I suspect, largely to your review!"

Once the eastern *Field Guide* was off and running, a western companion was clearly called for. But Roger had a nine-to-five job with the National Audubon Society in New York. Eventually he agreed to break loose and depend for his living on his royalties. By the time the western guide was published in 1941, the obvious question had occurred to all of us: If the "Peterson System" works for birds, can it be applied to other fields of natural history? Roger wrote to me in the spring of that year: "I have been giving considerable thought to the future extension of the series, and will be glad to discuss this more fully soon." He would be overall editor. Between us we would ferret out the leading authority on each subject, and an artist to match. (Few, like Roger, were both.) Most of these specialists were already overworked. They liked the concept, but I doubt that many of them had the remotest idea of what they were getting in for.

Haltingly, the series got under way. Progress on the first volume we contracted for — Margaret McKenny's *Field Guide to Wildflowers* — was scarcely encouraging. Begun in 1941, it was not published until 1968, rewritten and illustrated by Roger himself shortly before the original author's death. Roger's fame as a bird man has overshadowed his skill in other fields, including botany. Each spring he would drive around the countryside, seeking the flower he wanted in bloom, painting it in all its freshness that night in his motel. For years the book was "almost finished" — just a few species missing, which he had not found at the proper moment, to be added the next spring. When at last the book was on the market, its sales surpassed every other volume in the series except the bird guides. Even the professional botanists accepted it. A friend of mine, an expert on New England flora, had pooh-poohed the idea of such a book from the start: OK for birds, but wildflowers were too complicated. When he saw the finished product, he gave in with good grace.

Not all the titles in the series had quite such a long and troubled period of gestation. But none came easy. They are more than tools for identification. Many of them have made an important scientific contribution in their field. Today as I look at that long shelf of bright blue jackets numbered from 1 to 32 — and still growing — I wonder at the amount of talent and dogged labor that went into this enterprise. A mirror image of the ancient alchemists who sought to change base metal into gold, these field guide authors have been painstakingly converting their hard-earned and precious knowledge into common currency for use by us all. When the process seemed maddeningly slow, we could take comfort from a favorite saying of the African Zulus: "Patience is an egg that hatches great birds."

Not even an alchemist can work alone; someone must stoke the furnace. At Park Street the Grand Wizard (more formally known as chief copy editor) was Helen Phillips, whose job it was to prepare these complex, cross-referenced, double-distilled manuscripts for the printer: the literary equivalent of driving a forty-mule team. When I think of the *Field Guides*, I see Helen in her little corner office overlooking the Granary Burying Ground, surrounded by precariously balanced piles of carefully organized clutter. Every month or so Roger could be found at her elbow, having just arrived by early morning train from his home in Connecticut. An owl rather than a lark, he would not yet be fully awake, often belaboring some irrelevant subject while Helen gently but firmly brought him back to the matter at hand.

Essential to the whole *Field Guide* operation was Barbara, Roger's wife at the time. They have since gone their separate ways, but during those wonderfully productive years she was a true partner. In her own words she "kept the factory running." She answered his mountains of mail, made his appointments, managed his working schedule, ran his movie projector, and — bless her — kept in contact with his publisher. A naturalist in her own right, she received an award from The New York Zoological Society for her contributions in the field of ecology and natural history. And though I heard little mention of Barbara during the fiftieth anniversary celebrations, Roger has consistently acknowledged his debt to her, beginning with the dedication of the *Field Guide to Western Birds* over forty years ago.

When I think of Barbara, two scenes come to mind, both during a trip to Baja California with a group of scientists, organized by the late Kenneth Bechtel. My wife and I were in a small boat with Roger and Barbara when the propeller of our outboard motor struck a snag, breaking the shear-pin. The boatman had no spare. "If someone will go back to the motel," said Barbara, "and look in the upper left-hand drawer of my bureau, he will find my tool kit, with some shear-pins in it." Of course.

Later, on that same expedition, we visited an offshore island teeming with pelicans and boobies. In my mind's eye I see a narrow ledge where Roger has his camera focused on a Blue-footed Booby standing beside its nest, its powder-blue webbed feet brilliant against the gray rock. Behind him awaits Barbara, loaded down with further equipment to hand him as the filming proceeds.

For Roger, field trips were a glorious compensation for the steady grind of turning out the *Field Guides* that made him rich and famous. In a way he had become a prisoner of his own maturing talent. I remember an occasion many years ago when Houghton Mifflin was making yet another printing of *A Field Guide to the Birds*, which had last been revised in 1946. I complained to our art director that some of the color plates seemed poorly printed. "It's not our fault," he replied. "Take a look at the original paintings." I did. They were faithfully reproduced. I had been misled by the startling improvement in Roger's skill as an artist since the nineteen forties. Already he was well along with the climactic final revision published in 1980: an entirely new book, which gave full opportunity for his talent.

No, not quite. All along, Roger had yearned to create bird paintings solely as works of art, not just tools for identification. He has had many opportunities, including magazine publication. But his chief outlet has been his superb series of prints. Roger has always been competitive. He is generous in his praise of bird artists whom he admires; yet he is disturbed by the thought that some of these younger men may be getting ahead of him. What really burned him up was the claim of the late Robert Cushman Murphy, the Grand Old Man of the American Museum of Natural History, that there had been no great American bird artist since Audubon.

Roger's sense of competition is not confined to the field of painting. He is justly proud of his skill as a wildlife photographer, recording his adventures in the uttermost parts of the earth. How many scientists have seen and photographed all seventeen species of penguins? And how many birders have such a long "life list"? From the beginning he has considered bird watching a sport as well as a scientific occupation — clearly one reason for its vast popularity. He is delightfully single-minded. Only Roger would have scheduled a trip with his British colleague James Fisher — joint author of *Wild America* — to begin at Concord's North Bridge on the nineteenth of April, smack in the middle of the annual celebration of the "embattled farmers'" victory over the redcoats in 1775. The date meant nothing to him. James was in his element. "Tally ho!" cried that ebullient Englishman as he added one species after another to his life list; "Tally *very* ho!" When they spotted a Rusty Blackbird, which they feared they might miss as they traveled south. *Wild America*,

incidentally, is an example of Roger's versatility: the black-and-white drawings rank with his finest work. Best of all, it gave him a chance to write.

Of his many creative skills, the act of writing probably gives Roger the greatest pleasure. Back in 1950 he won the John Burroughs Medal (awarded annually for the best literary work in the field of natural history) for his *Birds Over America*. He continues to welcome every writing assignment that his full schedule permits. Regularly he would send me a glassine envelope containing a dozen neatly typed pages, each describing a book project that he was eager to undertake before someone else had the same idea. Meanwhile competition for his time kept growing. One formidable competitor with Houghton Mifflin for his talents was Lars-Eric Lindblad, who recruited Roger as naturalist on the cruise ship *Explorer*. Here Roger could make the most of his skill as a teacher, while enjoying a free ride to parts of the globe seldom visited. These trips were the perfect antidote for the fatigue of the paint pot and the drawing board. And their therapeutic value was enhanced by the ill-concealed admiration of an eager and appreciative audience.

When the current edition of the *Field Guide* finally appeared in 1980 it included an incomparable series of "range maps," showing where each species can be found in summer, in winter, or as a permanent resident. These are the work of Virginia Marie Peterson, Roger's long-time friend and neighbor in Old Lyme, Connecticut, whom he married in 1976. A professional biochemist, Ginny is the author of a guidebook for the U.S. Coast Guard and a pioneer in the technique of identifying the source of oil spills by infrared spectroscopy. Although I never had the pleasure of working with Ginny, I know that she devotes full time to "keeping the factory running" — a responsibility that includes the home, the studio, the office, and the staff. And since their marriage, she has traveled six continents with Roger, photographing wildlife. Currently they are working on the new *Field Guide to Western Birds*. She shares his enthusiasms: to take one example among many, she is a "penguin addict," as he noted in the dedication to her of his book on these appealing and photogenic birds. What better criterion for a happy and productive union?

ॐ

Widespread public recognition during one's lifetime can turn an individual into an institution, and one's name into a trademark. Few of us need worry about this. If Roger is aware of it, he doesn't let it bother him. I recall being on a bird walk with him when he was momentarily unsure of an identification. He turned to the group: "Does anyone have a 'Peterson' on him?"

Having known and admired Roger long before a "Peterson" meant a book, I am glad to add a grace note to the drums and sounding trumpets that, in 1984, celebrated the fiftieth birthday of the *Field Guide to the Birds* as a national event, with banquets, speeches, retrospective exhibitions, testimonials, plaques of bronze and plaques of wood inscribed with immortal words of praise, enough to fill a trophy room, to be added to Roger's collection of medals from all over the world. These festivities reached a climax when the Smithsonian Institution in Washington invited 350 guests to a dinner in the high-ceilinged hall of the National Museum of Natural History, where they dined beneath a charging bull elephant — as if to remind Roger that *his* collection of trophies was, by comparison, quite manageable.

The Peterson Field Guides have made publishing history. Altogether they have sold almost ten million copies, not counting translations of the European bird guide. And there has been a greater reward than any of us anticipated: the part these books have played in the international conservation movement. Recognition is the first step toward preservation. Every birder, for example, becomes to some degree an ecologist. In political terms he is a conservationist. When Roger Peterson was awarded the Gold Medal of the Société d'Acclimation, the citation credited him with "doing more in France than anyone else to interest people in birds; and, for nature conservation, anyone else in the world."

This citation brings to mind a comment by Elliot Richardson, whom Roger taught at Rivers School and "tutored" occasionally during summer vacations. His greatest contribution, Richardson feels, is in enlarging our awareness. "He is one of those people who feel the need to give, who are filled with an enthusiasm which they long to share."

The most recent product of this shared enthusiasm is the founding of the Peterson Institute for the Study of Natural History, in Roger's home town of Jamestown, New York — a by-product, as he says, of the Field Guide Series, which will carry on his work both in America and abroad.

6
Ross and Tom
A Footnote

T HIS BRIEF CHAPTER is a personal footnote to a long book entitled *Ross and Tom: Two American Tragedies* written by John Leggett, at one time publicity director at Park Street, later a successful novelist. "Ross" is Ross Lockridge, author of *Raintree County*, published in 1948; "Tom" is Thomas Heggen, whose *Mister Roberts* appeared two years earlier. Both writers killed themselves at the height of their sudden success. In re-creating the whole sad story with a novelist's insight, Jack Leggett was not drawing on personal experience of dealing with the two authors; he had not yet joined the Houghton Mifflin staff when their books were published. I had, however, given him free access to our correspondence files, to quote as he saw fit. It was therefore a rather unnerving experience to read his well-documented account of events during the nine months of turmoil preceding *Raintree County*'s birth. I turned the pages gingerly. After a quarter of a century, did my memory fit the facts?

Considered purely as a publishing operation, *Raintree County* had everything: selection of the Book-of-the-Month Club, a major motion picture prize, advance excerpt in *Life* magazine, and, two months after publication, number one position on the fiction best-seller list. But no book I can remember experienced such birth pains. And none had a more tragic outcome.

The original typescript of Lockridge's huge opus arrived at Park Street in five thick folders, each the dimension of a full-length novel. Readers' reactions were mixed. But a feeling of excitement ran through the office. For all its unwieldy size, its seemingly ungoverned exuberance, it was obviously a work of immense talent and of unlimited ambition. A volcanic explosion of words, it obviously needed editing, including drastic cutting. There is where the trouble began.

Ross did not underestimate his achievement. Though he must have felt a kinship with Thomas Wolfe, he saw himself more in a class with Thomas Mann and James Joyce — convinced, however, that his novel "goes beyond *Ulysses*." This caused problems when, as a first step, we had to persuade him to discard most of folder number five, which was a Joycean "stream of consciousness": an interminable dreamlike coda following completion of the story proper. Retained as it stood, it would have sunk the book. But this haunting incantation was, understandably, dear to the author's heart. He realized the necessity, but it hurt him to throw it overboard.

Cutting the story itself down to size was another matter. (The printed book would still be over a thousand pages.) The hero of this operation was senior editor Craig Wylie, who expressed faith in Lockridge from the start, and through his editing made the publication possible.

For Ross this experience had been painful enough. But it was not yet over. When at last the galley proofs were ready, a pattern began to emerge which, in retrospect, set the tone for everything that followed: one triumph after another, each shadowed by fresh anxiety and pain.

The first was the most spectacular and the most painful. Metro-Goldwyn-Mayer offered a prize of $150,000 for motion picture rights to a novel, with the idea of attracting new talent to their studio and, they hoped, riding on the coattails of a best seller. Dorothy de Santillana, our managing editor, suggested to Ross that he enter the contest. He did, and he won. But only if he agreed to further cuts. He was reluctant. MGM's agent, Carol Brandt, was tough and unshakable. Obviously she was afraid the book would fail and the movie along with it. Money won, and he gave in. He was assured of his prize.

But that was not the end of it. Late one Friday afternoon in July, after the office was officially closed, I had a call from MGM's New York office. They had decided, they said, to split the first prize between *Raintree County* and another novel and were going to announce this in the Monday morning papers. Fortunately I had a copy of the MGM announcement of the contest in my desk drawer. It specifically stated that there would be one — and only one — first prize. I got Ross on the phone. Though he had only an oral commitment from MGM, we decided to go for all or nothing. In a three-way hookup with their office, I read from their own statement of the contest rules, hung up, and awaited the Monday morning papers with some trepidation. Lockridge was announced the winner. A "special prize" was awarded to the other author. Was it possible that the movie magnates placed their call after hours on Friday with the expectation that there would be no answer, and that they could proceed with their plan to get the rights of two books for the price of one?

By midsummer all that was over. Success seemed assured. But MGM's demands for massive cuts were hard to meet. Tension was building up, and finally it burst out in an odd direction. A New York lawyer whom he had met through MGM encouraged Ross to believe that Houghton Mifflin was cheating him by taking the usual agent's fee on the motion picture rights — ignoring the fact that we had already saved him from giving up half of his prize. His letters became abusive; he would have nothing more to do with Houghton Mifflin in the future, etcetera, etcetera. Finally I had had too much. I wrote telling him — in polite but emphatic terms — to reconsider; we had done very well for him.

At home in Lincoln the following Sunday morning I received a collect call from Manistee, Michigan. Ross had my letter. He now realized that he had been badly advised. He went on to apologize earnestly and lengthily for his behavior, while I assured him that we understood, and all was well. Such misunderstandings, I lied, were routine. He hung up at last, apparently satisfied.

But during breakfast on Monday he called again. I reminded him that we had settled all this yesterday. Yes, he said, but when you get to your office you will find a letter from me written before I received yours; I want you to promise me to destroy it unread. Routine, I replied in effect. Eventually he hung up, assured. When I reached my office, a fat, sealed letter lay on my desk. Then followed the only rewarding moment in this tedious sequence. I took the unopened letter to the office of our sales manager, Hardwick Moseley. He knew that much of the year's sales would depend on Lockridge's book, he knew of the trouble I had been having with him, but he knew nothing of the weekend telephone conversations. "I've had enough of this," I said, showing Hardwick the unopened letter. "I don't care whether we publish him or not." Whereupon I tore the letter into shreds and dropped them into his wastebasket. His expression at that moment remains vivid after almost forty years.

From that time onward, all went well. Advance sales were splendid. The initial reviews were prominent and favorable. Author and publisher were in complete accord. My last communication with Ross was my telegram early in the new year, informing him that *Raintree County* stood number one on the *New York Times* best-seller list. The next thing I heard, he was dead.

It would take a full-length book — and has — to get to the roots of this disaster. I know that Ross was trying, and failing, to get started on another novel. His dream had been realized. Would the rest of his life be an anticlimax? And I think that he had been hurt by some of the later reviews, which mocked his effusive style and failed to award him the rank he felt he deserved.

Speaking of reviews, it was a trifle ironic to have more than one critic suggest that *Raintree County* would have been a better novel if the author had had an editor like Maxwell Perkins (Wolfe's famous mentor at Scribners) to make him do some cutting! On the other hand *The Writer* magazine, following his suicide, published an open letter: "Dear Mr. Brooks: You have killed your author" — by making him cut his manuscript. Sometimes you can't win.

ॐ

Like Ross Lockridge, Tom Heggen was the victim of the immediate overwhelming success of his first book — *Mister Roberts* — followed by doubts that such a triumph could ever be repeated. This, of course, is a vast oversimplification; as Jack Leggett made clear, their "self-constructed hells" were very different from each other. So were the two young men: Ross, manic, ebullient, lacking a sense of humor that would have made him hesitate to compare himself with Shakespeare; Tom, shy, wryly humorous, naturally bawdy, and satiric. When I returned from Europe in the fall of 1945, his manuscript was already in the office, having been sent to Dorothy de Santillana by Heggen's cousin, Wallace Stegner, newly appointed literary scout for Houghton Mifflin. The short novel in manuscript, consisting of a number of related episodes (which reached a climax when Mr. Roberts threw the captain's cherished palm tree overboard), was entitled "The Iron-Bound Bucket" — the derisive sobriquet used by Tom's shipmates aboard the troop transport in the Pacific. Unless one knew the background, this title didn't mean much, nor did it strike us as particularly appealing. Why not call it *Mister Roberts*? He was the central character who held together what was essentially a book of short stories. And the "Mister" suggested the naval setting. Tom instantly agreed.

Unlike Ross, Tom made no claims for his little book, and I think he had honest doubts. But further assurance came when I sent galleys to the *Atlantic;* they took three chapters and awarded him an "Atlantic First." And as I learned later from Henry Canby, the Book-of-the-Month Club judges would probably have chosen it if it had ever reached them. Alas, their head reader, Amy Loveman, was offended by some of the four-letter words and threw it out.

One scene from this pre-publication period sticks in my memory: the sales conference luncheon to which we customarily invited one or two current authors (in this case, John Dos Passos and Tom Heggen) to say a few words. After adequate food and drink — and assurances from me that this was all very informal — Tom arose in obvious distress, tried to smile, tried to speak, and sat down. As if to comfort him, Dos stood up in his turn, squirmed, stuttered, mumbled a word or two, and sat down. We should have known better.

Another moment I recall was meeting Tom at the stage door after the wildly successful opening of *Mister Roberts* on Broadway. The book by then was famous, and Tom's traumatic experience of turning it into a play with the collaboration of Joshua Logan — while keeping his own identity as author — was presumably all behind him. Cries of "Author! Author!" had filled the theater as the curtain went down. Logan, as I recall it, appeared briefly on stage. But no Tom, though his face had been made up in anticipation of going on. I thought at the time that it was mere shyness that held him back. But apparently it went deeper than that. *Mister Roberts* was his creation. During the writing of the play he had felt it slipping from his hands. He was the author, and he was not going to share that with anyone. Later that evening, by now feeling no pain, he mingled with the guests at a first-night party packed with celebrities, a bottle of whiskey tucked under his arm.

The theatrical world and steamy nightclubs of New York made an unnourishing atmosphere for future work. Estranged from his wife, involved with an overlapping sequence of beautiful and adoring women, seeking surcease from pain in alcohol and massive doses of drugs, Tom would face the blank page in his typewriter. Unable to begin another book, he was haunted by the thought that *Mister Roberts* may have been a lucky fluke, that perhaps he was not a writer after all. This, of course, is hindsight. So far as I recall, none of us at Park Street knew how desperate the situation had become. Innocently, we were looking forward to his future work when we learned that he had committed suicide. Had we been aware of the hell that he was going through, we might have realized that not even his matchless sense of humor could have saved him.

7
Nature Writers and Artists

WHEN ROGER PETERSON BRISTLED at Bob Murphy's remark that there have been no great American bird artists since Audubon, he doubtless had in mind, above all others, Louis Agassiz Fuertes. "To the strictly ornithological clan," Roger has written, "Fuertes' name stands without peer, placed way ahead of Audubon." Leaving aside comparisons, it's good to know that today, after so many years, Fuertes's work is getting the recognition it deserves. A recent exhibition of his paintings at the Academy of Natural Sciences was jammed with enthusiasts, Roger prominent among them.

What has this to do with Park Street? Shift the scene up the hill to the State House and the time to the late nineteen thirties. During the previous decade the Commonwealth of Massachusetts had published a work of natural history that quickly became a classic: the three-volume *Birds of Massachusetts and Other New England States* by Edward Howe Forbush, illustrated in color by Louis Agassiz Fuertes (later joined by Allan Brooks). Forbush — who died just before the third volume was completed — had been an eminent and adventurous ornithologist with a quiet sense of humor and a charming literary style: the patron saint of New England birders. Like many earlier nature writers, he saw no reason why the audience for a scientific work should be confined to scientists. Everything he wrote is highly readable. But three fat volumes were quite an investment for the average book buyer. And anyway, one of them was already out of print. Would the state authorities, we wondered, give Houghton Mifflin the right to publish an abridged one-volume edition at a price the general public could afford?

I called on the Secretary of State: a pleasant, no-nonsense gentleman who had apparently held that office since before the Flood. Yet this was probably his first official encounter with birds and their passionate admirers. The State, as we both knew, was not empowered to make a deal with a commercial company; but we planned to get around that by acting through the Massachusetts Audubon Society. Fine, except that the Society's president had already raised some hackles in the State House by his regal manner. Fortunately he was no longer in charge of negotiations. In no time at all the Secretary and I had drafted a one-page agreement that seemed to cover everything.

Or so we thought. But I soon heard from the governor's "legal advisor." Our agreement, it appeared, was offensively simple. Where, for example, were the mandatory "WHEREAS's," establishing the existence of the Commonwealth of Massachusetts, of Houghton Mifflin Company, of birds? Who were the parties of the first part and of the second part? And so on. Back I go to another office in the State House for three long sessions with this lawyer, worrying over the wording of a multipage document. At last we are done. The "legal advisor" rolls his damp — but fortunately dead — cigar from left to right for the last time. He sighs, "Well, we lawyers are used to this sort of thing." I must have looked surprised. "Aren't you a lawyer?" he asked. This, I believe, is the only time I have been mistaken for a member of the bar.

We now had the publishing rights. Dr. John B. May, who had completed Forbush's great work, abridged his text and added more than one hundred species, extending the book's range to cover the entire territory east of the ninety-fifth meridian. Roger Peterson illustrated these additional species in four new color plates. We changed the title to *Natural History of the Birds of Eastern and Central North America*.

Francis Allen, who had shepherded the Peterson *Field Guide* through the press, did the same for the one-volume Forbush. This process had its dramatic moments. Dr. May was competent, but choleric. One day he and Mr. Allen got into a fierce argument over the "song" of the American Bittern, which utters

"peculiar love notes like the sound of a wooden pump."
They agreed to render the three notes as "ugh-plum-pud'n," but they couldn't agree on the accent. "Ugh-*PLUM*-pud'n!" shouted Dr. May for the last time as, red in the face, he stomped down the stairs of Two Park Street, threatening to abandon the job and go to Alaska. Mr. Allen, generally so mild in manner, roared down the stairwell as May departed: "Ugh-plum-PUD'N"! (Forbush himself lists twenty renditions of the Bittern's pumping note, ranging from "punc-a-pog" to "walker-ker-toot." "I doubt," he comments, "if the bird uses any.")

Published in 1939, *Natural History of the Birds* became an anchor book on our nature list: the birder's perfect companion to the *Field Guide*. Peterson in your pocket, Forbush on the back seat.

ॐ

For well over a century, nature writers have found a home at Park Street. This is doubtless owing in part to our long ownership of the *Atlantic Monthly*, which published a nature essay in its first issue in 1857 and continued to welcome such articles for approximately a century, through the editorship of Ted Weeks. (Thereafter the magazine would occasionally publish a piece on wilderness or conservation, but it had to be both "newsworthy" and controversial.) I suppose that the most enduring nature writer to come to Houghton Mifflin via the *Atlantic* was John Muir, during the editorship of Walter Hines Page. Page was the sort of editor authors dream of. When Muir apologized to him for the delay in delivering copy of books on Alaska and the National Parks, he replied: "I thank God that you do not write in glib, acrobatic fashion . . . The two books . . . will not need any special season's sales, any other accidental circumstances. They'll be Literature!" Like those Zulus, Page knew the value of patience. It's a pity that he and Muir — founder of the Sierra Club — cannot see the influence in our time of the eggs they so patiently hatched.

Nowadays everybody is writing about John Muir — biographies, interpretations, selections from his text to give weight to photograph books (which, being interpreted, means providing enough reading matter to cause the potential bookstore customer to feel uneasy about simply looking at the pictures and replacing the book on the counter). An example from our list: *Yosemite and the Sierra Nevada*, selected from Muir's writings, featuring photographs — excuse me, "images" — by Ansel Adams. This was published in 1948. Two years later we sponsored a similar marriage of like minds: Ansel Adams illustrating Mary Austin's *The Land of Little Rain*. We also published Ansel's (and Edward Weston's) early albums. All of this led to a lasting friendship with Ansel and his wife, Virginia — who must be one of the most beloved women in the State of California.

Ansel Adams's last great retrospective volume,

Yosemite and the Range of Light (for which I wrote
the introductory essay), was published by the New
York Graphic Society in 1979 — over thirty years after
our book with an almost identical title. "The Range of
Light" was John Muir's phrase for the Sierra Nevada.
There could not be a better one for the special talent of
the great photographer himself.

ॐ

April 1940 found me with Susan in California, halfway
through an eight-week editorial "scouting trip" to see
new authors and to visit several already on the list.
(Though I took many trips alone, Susie's presence
added both to the pleasure of such journeys, and to the
results.) We had joined the spring as it moved up from
the south, followed it north and west. Now in Santa
Barbara we were to meet a newcomer to the Houghton
Mifflin nature list: Donald Culross Peattie. Still in his
early forties (which didn't seem so young to us), he
had become one of the most popular literary naturalists
of his generation.

We were welcomed by his wife, a successful novelist
who had published under her maiden name, Louise
Redfield. Handsome, self-assured, she looked at me
with evident surprise: "I thought you would be older."
"Did you think I would have long white whiskers?"
"Of course. Doesn't Santa Claus have long white
whiskers?" The reason for her cordial retort was the
recent publication of *Audubon's America:* a volume of
John J. Audubon's engaging but little-known writings,

illustrated with some of the best reproductions so far made of his prints and paintings. I had suggested this somewhat obvious project to her husband, whose well-known name, appearing as editor, would guarantee a good sendoff. His job had not been onerous, and now the royalties were pouring in. Since the material was no longer in copyright, they poured straight down the chimney of the house in Santa Barbara.

Presently the high double doors of the living room swung open. A tall (Don Peattie was a Scot), mild-mannered man made his well-staged entrance. So began a long friendship, resulting in the publication of book after book on nature, naturalists, and his enthusiastic — if somewhat rose-tinted — interpretation of the American continent and its history. (He was, for instance, more authoritative in dealing with the Passenger Pigeon than with the romanticized "Bird Woman," Sacajawea, the young squaw who led Lewis and Clark to the Pacific.)

Don Peattie was a gentle soul. His style was more that of W. H. Hudson than of John Muir. One can't imagine him, like Muir, climbing to the top of a tall Douglas fir in the Sierra to experience the full force of a mountain storm, or glorying in an earthquake while the floor of Yosemite Valley shook beneath his feet and huge chunks of rock crashed down from the cliffs above his head. Don's totem was St. Francis of Assisi, whose stone image presided over the birdbath in his garden — which in turn provided the title for a charming book of essays, *A Cup of Sky*. Like many of our best nature writers, he could afford an emotional response without departing from the facts.

Don's love of nature and the English language never dimmed his sharp eye for the dollar. His affable but tough New York agent, George Bye, who specialized in national celebrities, was sometimes too busy to mind the niceties. For example, he once thoughtlessly forwarded to me a letter from Don demanding higher royalties: if Brooks wouldn't pay them, wrote the gentle author, some other publisher would. Rose petals and greenbacks blended smoothly in the Peatties' world — notably when Don joined the payroll of the *Reader's Digest*. But at his best, dealing with natural history — especially his major subject of botany — he was an ornament to a great tradition. His two volumes on the *Natural History of the Trees*, east and west, illustrated with woodcuts by Paul Landacre, bear somewhat the same relation to the *Field Guide to the Trees* that Forbush does to the *Field Guide to the Birds*. Though popular rather than technical, they are worthy of the publishers of Sargent's *Manual*.

And through an odd chain of circumstances, *Audubon's America* was in part responsible for our publishing John Kieran, Bernard De Voto, and Winston Churchill. More of that later.

Have you ever been fly fishing on snowshoes? Susie and I enjoyed this bizarre experience on the Snake River in Jackson Hole, Wyoming, during the trip home.

Our hosts were those fabulous twin naturalists, Frank and John Craighead, co-authors of *Hawks in the Hand* (HMCo, 1939). At work on a *Field Guide to Rocky Mountain Wildflowers*, they had asked for an editorial conference, and I had suggested the first days of May, the opening of the trout fishing season.

After leaving the Peatties in Santa Barbara we had continued north: in Olympia meeting Margaret McKenny, also engaged on a field guide, and from Seattle making the first of many trips to the Olympic Peninsula, where a great national park had recently been born. At the University of Washington we had the good fortune to meet Theodore Roethke, whose poetry is so deeply rooted in wild nature. Thence we headed east. By the end of April we were approaching Jackson Hole National Monument.

All my previous correspondence had been addressed simply to "The Craigheads, Moose, Wyoming." The replies were invariably in the first person plural. But this last Christmas we had received two cards: (1) a photo of Frank and a pretty blonde, on snowshoes outside a log cabin, (2) a photo of John and a pretty brunette outside another log cabin. There was more going on here than identifying wildflowers.

Though I had wired ahead to announce our coming, the snow cover in the valley was three feet deep, and I had no idea whether or not my telegram had made it to their cabins. But soon after passing Moose we spotted a pair of snowshoes upended beside the road. We were expected. A quick change for me from low shoes to boots, a short walk on the snowshoes to Frank and Esther's cabin, and back with a pair for Susie. (The white kid gloves packed in her boots suggested the variety of these editorial trips.)

Frank and John, identical twins, had always done everything together. At Penn State they had both been on the wrestling team — which must have been confusing to the spectators. Together they had written an article for *National Geographic Magazine* on falconry, which led to a visit with a sport-loving prince in India. They collaborated on their doctoral dissertations at the University of Michigan. (Later, during World War II, they would receive identical citations for their joint authorship of a U.S. Navy handbook, *Survival on Land and Sea.*) Nor did matrimony change the pattern. When we met at the cabin door, Susie instantly recognized that Esther was pregnant. Yes, she was expecting in August. Next morning we met John's Margaret. The same, precisely. When we returned home I wrote a stern letter to "The Craigheads," reminding them of their tradition of joint production. In August — having long since forgotten about the matter — we received a single postcard, headed BIRTHS. They had made it the same day, with fifteen minutes to spare.

Driving through Jackson Hole today, bumper-to-bumper during the tourist season, it's hard to picture the same spot in 1940. The trout, the curious cow-moose in our front yard, the moose calf near death from starvation at winter's end, Frank climbing a tall conifer to look into an active hawk's nest, breaking off the dead

limbs close to the trunk with a quick blow of the hand
to make footholds. (He made it look as easy as mounting a ladder.) These stick in my memory. But best of
all was the day we floated down the Snake River from
Moose to Jackson in two tiny rubber rafts: Frank and
I in one, John and Susie in the other. The twins were
making a survey of Canada goose nests on the gravel
bars, to determine whether sudden release of water from
a dam upstream was flooding them out. If you have ever
run rapids in a canoe, you can imagine the sensation of
floating down them backwards and sideways. Our
friends had sharp eyes. As we drifted down on an
apparently lifeless bar, a quiet voice announces: "I
think I see a feather!" We land. Sure enough, there in
the gravel is a well-concealed goose nest.

Noon found us in Jackson, warming up in a diner-car
with a sandwich and a shot of whiskey. For Susie and
me, the trip had been a sample of natural history field-
work at its most benign.

It is not always thus. The Craigheads' laboratory is
the outdoors, the ruggeder the better. Photographs show
them being attacked on a sheer rock cliff by a Prairie
Falcon, and descending on a rope from a Bald Eagle's
nest high above the earth. When someone asked them
about such risks, the answer was simply "What better
way to go?"

Fortunately for us, they haven't gone. Today they
are famous for — among other things — their pioneer-
ing studies in the life history of the grizzly bear, using
modern techniques of tranquilizing darts and radio

transmitters to achieve a shocking invasion of privacy of which the subjects are fortunately unaware, and which have provided information essential to their preservation. Frank tells the story in *Track of the Grizzly* (Sierra Club Books, 1979). "I have always felt," he writes in his preface, "that the scientist has an obligation to explain his work and findings to the general public as well as to other scientists." This he and John have accomplished with rare success, in articles, in films, in books; through universities, government agencies, and conservation organizations, and through passing along their spirit and skills to later generations of Craigheads who have grown up in their outdoor world.

In natural history, as in any other special field, one author leads to another. At Park Headquarters in Jackson Hole we met Olaus Murie, director of the Wilderness Society and one of America's great mammalogists. He admired the Peterson *Field Guides* and agreed to contribute a volume covering one of the many subjects on which he was expert: animal tracks. An artist and writer as well as a scientist, he could, like Roger Peterson, provide both text and illustration. And like Frank Craighead, he felt an obligation to share his knowledge and skills with the rest of us. "Who lives in the forest?" he would write in the introduction to his book. "What creatures inhabit the banks of streams, the shores of lakes, or the sands of the desert? What are the animals that leave footprints in the mud, and trails in the snow? What has gnawed the bark, or clipped the twig?"

A Field Guide to Animal Tracks, published thirteen years later, was an instant success. It had survived a minor crisis when Olaus fell ill with two drawings still to be done. At Park Street we created the footprint of a caribou from a mounted hoof in a local museum, and I provided a drawing of an ancient blaze on a tree to complete the illustrations.

The Muries, like the Craigheads, came in pairs. Another summer, when Susie and I were in Alaska, we stopped to see Olaus's younger brother Adolph, author of the classic *Wolves of Mt. McKinley*. The Muries were living in Mt. McKinley National Park studying grizzly bears and Dall sheep. These sheep — pure white, smaller and slenderer than their darker cousins to the south, the Bighorns — are, like them, creatures of the mountaintops. As I wrote later in *Roadless Area:* to be introduced to Dall sheep by the Murie brothers was like being introduced to St. Peter by the Pope. That morning we climbed up a steep talus slope in short bursts, pausing frequently to catch our breath. The wind at our back crackled with a sound like that of tearing paper, and the odor of sage was in the air. Adolph, I am convinced, knew where the sheep would be before they knew themselves. Reaching the summit of the ridge, we peeked cautiously around a huge boulder and looked an old ram straight in the eye. Unperturbed, he and his younger companions lay down on the nearby grass slope

while we ate our sandwiches within a few yards of
them. Then we moved on, concerned that we might be
occupying their favorite spot in the sun.

All of which may seem a far cry from Two Park
Street. But one must keep in touch with one's authors.

કૈ

Trips away from one's desk may also help in acquiring
new writers, more by luck than by design. When Sally
Carrighar, famous for her books on animal behavior
and life in the arctic, decided to change publishers,
there was strong competition for her future work. Our
bid was doubtless strengthened by the fact that Susie
and I had read her last book out loud above the Arctic
Circle. (I was gathering material for a magazine article
opposing Edward Teller's mad scheme for testing atom
bombs under the guise of creating a harbor in North-
west Alaska.) And Jane Goodall, author of that capti-
vating study of wild chimpanzees, *In the Shadow of
Man*, may possibly have felt more at home at Two Park
Street because I had at least a nodding acquaintance
with East African animals.

Enough, you'll say, about nature writers. Save us
from a list like the "begats" in the Bible. But I must
mention a few more. James Fisher, whom Roger
Tory Peterson identified as "The Roger Tory Peterson
of England." James's friend Peter Scott, son of Robert
Scott of South Pole fame, and his country's best known
naturalist. Back home there was John Kieran, whom
I persuaded — "lashed me into it" was his phrase — to

write *A Natural History of New York City;* and later, with no need of the lash, his autobiography.

Dillon Ripley (the former secretary of the Smithsonian), Louis Halle (diplomat and ornithologist), Konrad Lorenz (the great animal behaviorist), Joseph Wood Krutch (drama critic turned naturalist), Robert Cushman Murphy (still active at the American Museum of Natural History), and Edwin Way Teale (dean of American nature writers) appeared at least once or twice on our list. For staying power and awesome production, the champion is probably Guy Murchie, who was already a familiar (and towering) figure when I arrived at Park Street, and who would, like the philosophers of old, take all science as his province.

As for the impact of these many writers on the course of history, the palm goes to Rachel Carson. More of her later; she is in a category by herself.

8
The English Connection

O<small>N RETURNING</small> from an editorial scouting trip, one writes for one's colleagues a long and glowing report on the talent one has encountered, on the manuscripts that will soon be flowing in. Some do, eventually. But results are to be measured in terms not of weeks or months, but of years.

From time immemorial, the London Trip has been a tradition and a highly valued perk of American trade publishers. In earlier days it was, I suspect, largely a matter of one-way traffic, with American publishers seeking British authors more ardently than London publishers sought talent here. (Even in my time there seemed to be a lingering impression among our London counterparts that New York and Boston, though no longer colonial towns, were socially still on the frontier. Witness the fact that, while the American visitor was always expected to dress for dinner in London, his

English colleague seldom brought dinner clothes to America.)

Ties between Park Street and the London publishing world have always been strong. When I arrived on the scene, several American publishers had working arrangements with compatible English firms. Ours was with the prestigious, if somewhat conservative, house of George Allen and Unwin, headed by Stanley Unwin, the highly respected panjandrum of the British book trade, author of *The Truth About Publishing*. The title was apt. Sir Stanley, as he later became, was a secure man, untroubled by doubts. When the time came for him to write his autobiography, he asked his nephew and successor, Philip Unwin, to read the manuscript before it went to press. Philip did so and expressed appropriate praise, but he suggested that his uncle might mention one or two occasions in a long and distinguished career when he had made an error of judgment. "But my dear Philip," the author protested, "we don't want any *fiction* in this book, do we?"

The Allen and Unwin connection did not strike many sparks. On one occasion, however, it lit a slow fire that smoldered for years before bursting into flame. The Unwin catalogue for 1937 listed, as usual, their new adult books followed by new juveniles, but there was no break to indicate where the former ended and the latter began. Either the last of the adult books or (more likely) the first of the juveniles was a volume entitled *The Hobbit*, by an Oxford don named J. R. R.

Tolkien. Proofs had routinely been submitted to HMCo, inviting an offer for American rights. Our managing editor (he then had charge of children's books) was not impressed. Nor was the children's librarian at the Boston Public Library, whom we asked for a professional opinion. Yet for some reason — though I know nothing about juveniles — I read *The Hobbit* and fell for Mr. Bilbo Baggins and his crew. No matter what age this story was written for, we must give it a try. We did, and the *New York Herald Tribune* awarded it a prize for one of the best children's books of the season. The *New York Times* wrote: "This is a book with no age limits. All those, young or old, who love a finely imagined story, beautifully told, will take *The Hobbit* to their hearts."

By now generations of readers have done so. But sixteen years passed before Professor Tolkien launched *The Lord of the Rings*, the first volume of his now fabulous trilogy, which has been compared to the great epics of Western literature. Credit for recognizing its quality belongs largely to editor Anne Barrett. Her editorial report on the first volume, *The Fellowship of the Ring*, concluded: "A rich book and a deadly serious one. I think it is wonderful, but it has its drawbacks. Who will read 423 pages about an unfinished journey undertaken by mythical creatures with confusing names? Probably no one, but I still say it is wonderful and — with my heart in my mouth — *to publish*. October, 1953."

The subsequent volumes, *The Two Towers* and *The Return of the King*, followed only a year apart. Sales continued to mount throughout the sixties, a period when college-age youth was in eruption against the world they saw around them. Perhaps their longing for "a scrubbed morning world" (as one critic put it), for exciting adventure and heroic seriousness, was what led them to flock to Tolkien's imaginary Middle-earth, to set up Tolkien clubs throughout the land, to buy his books literally in the millions. At Park Street Anne Barrett became the authority on this priceless addition to our list, and, to Tolkien's delight, made a special trip to visit him in England. His posthumous book, *The Silmarillion*, published in 1977, sold over a million copies in hard cover.

ॐ

The Hobbit had been published in 1938. The previous year we brought out a book of another kind, also received from Allen and Unwin. It dealt with a world less believable than Middle-earth, but unfortunately real. The title was *My Battle* (*Mein Kampf*). The author, Adolf Hitler, was described in our bulletin as "the most powerful single personage in the world."

On the basis of readability, no publisher in his right mind would have published this book. The turgid prose — no doubt an accurate rendering of the original German — the ranting, the lack of organization, made it difficult to get through. But that was not the point.

Here, if one had the patience to dig it out, was an unequivocal statement of Hitler's beliefs and intentions. In the words of the distinguished columnist Dorothy Thompson, one of the first writers to warn Americans of the Nazi menace: "The reading of this book is a duty for all who would understand the fantastic era in which we live." Those who threatened to bomb the building if we published — and there were one or two "bomb scares" — failed to get the idea. So did those who later accused us of bringing out an abridged and "watered down" version of the original. At the time this was the only available translation, and time was of the essence. And as I recall from struggling with the text, the main points were there. Sales eventually exceeded a quarter of a million.

Five years later — in August 1942 — we published (in collaboration with Reynal & Hitchcock) a new and complete translation of *Mein Kampf* by Ralph Manheim, with an introduction by the leading authority on Hitler, Konrad Heiden. (Heiden once told me that he almost punched Hitler in the nose over some argument in a beer hall — and was now sorry he hadn't.)

About this same time another American publisher brought out a pirated translation of *Mein Kampf*, advertised with the boast: "No royalties to Hitler!" This was a specious claim: the publisher must have known that, in wartime, royalties earned by an enemy alien are paid to the Alien Property Custodian. Hitler never saw a cent of his American earnings. More important, by paying royalties according to contract, by adhering to the copyright law, we were defending the rights of refugees from Hitler's Germany, like Thomas and Heinrich Mann and many others, who depended on literary royalties for their livelihood. In due course we were granted an injunction terminating the sale of the pirated edition.

All of which reminds me of a dinner party many years later at Folly Farm, the country estate of Mr. and Mrs. Hugh Astor, whom I had come to know in connection with our publication of the *Times Atlas*. (The Astor family then owned *The Times* of London.) One of the guests was the distinguished Oxford historian, Hugh Trevor-Roper, author of *The Last Days of Hitler*. Over sherry he had held forth at length on his rôle in electing the new Chancellor of the University. But at dinner he was silent; my attempts at conversation fell flat. Finally I thought to mention our current search for the heir to Hitler's literary estate, presumably a niece. This got his attention. He assured me that he was the only authority on the subject, and proceeded to produce his evidence. Suddenly, in midsentence, he stopped. "I am giving you information of financial value, am I not?" and turned away. (The "financial value" still escapes me.) Later in the evening I asked him politely about his current work. "In the interests of self-protection," he replied, "I must decline to answer that question." Knowing his reputation, I should not have been surprised. But it didn't make for a jolly

party. As for Hitler's heir, the information he declined to give me has long since become irrelevant.

By the way, *The Times Atlas of the World* — which had led to my friendship with the Astors — was one of the enduring fruits of these rather chancy editorial trips to London. On one such trip I had made an arrangement with the brilliant, well-informed, and personable editor of the TLS (*Times Literary Supplement*), Alan Pryce-Jones, to act as a "literary scout" for Houghton Mifflin — to give us early warning of any book project that might have special interest for the American market. This had no immediate results. But one morning there arrived in the mail an advance copy of a brochure from *The Times* of London announcing a major publication: a new edition, in five volumes, of the famous *Times Atlas*. (Last published in 1928, in one volume.) With it was a note from Alan, suggesting that we might be interested in the American rights. An understatement. But, alas, the brochure stated that sales in America would be handled by the *Times* office in New York. I cabled Alan: IF THE BROCHURE HASN'T GONE OUT, HOLD IT. It hadn't, and he did. But in the year 1958 five volumes (to be published serially) at twenty-five dollars each was a lot of money. The sales manager was against it. Yet a few inquiries convinced us that there was nothing comparable on the market. If you know you have the best there is, the risk is worth taking. We imported sheets and bound them (in the bright red cloth beloved by Lovell Thompson). Each volume eventually sold out, and Volume III, *The Americas*, had to be reordered. In 1967 there was a one-volume edition. The risk paid off.

Of British historians other than the Hitler specialist, I have warmer memories. Among those published at Park Street were James Laver of the Victoria and Albert Museum, witty chronicler of Victorian and Edwardian England; J. B. Plumb, author of *The Four Georges* and biographer of England's first prime minister, Sir Robert Walpole (whose political philosophy, according to *1066 and All That*, was "*Quieta non movere:* let sleeping dogs lie"). There was that brilliant talker, teacher, and — when he found time for it — writer, Lord David

Cecil. There was Sir Arthur Bryant, whose three-volume *The Story of England* we published in the nineteen fifties. When I dined with him and his wife at their home in London, I inquired about a gold medal reposing on a table in their drawing room. "I am rather proud of that," he replied with British understatement. "It has been awarded only twice: once to Winston and once to me." In Windsor there was Georgina Battiscombe. When Susie and I first came to know her, she and her husband, Colonel Battiscombe, were living in the Henry III Tower of Windsor Castle, next door to the royal family; all night long, guards paced back and forth beneath our window. Years later, her friendship with her distinguished neighbors made possible her superb biography of Queen Alexandra.

Speaking of biography, few works in our time can match, in scope and scholarship, the definitive life of Winston Churchill. Begun with extraordinary competence by his son, Randolph, it has been continued, after Randolph's untimely death, by the recognized authority on Churchill, Martin Gilbert. As I write, it has reached six volumes, each growing stouter — and unlike most of us, even livelier — with the passing years. Seldom has a biographer been so completely absorbed in his subject. He remodeled his house in Oxford to be a sort of Churchill library. And according to one of Churchill's daughters, Gilbert's voice, when he reads aloud from her father's words, is so like her father's as to be almost eerie. The identification of one with the other is virtually complete.

One of the most immediately successful of our English authors was not the fruit of any trip to London. He came to us — or rather we came to him — from editor Austin Olney's desk at Park Street. Austin had spotted in the London *Economist* a shrewd and amusing article entitled "Parkinson's Law" ("Work expands so as to fill the time available for its completion"). Here, Austin recognized, was the germ of a book. The same principle — illustrated in this case by conditions in the Royal Navy — could be applied to other walks of life. He got in touch with the author, who agreed. So in due course we had a book by a British author, the British rights of which, by an odd reversal of circumstances, we then proceeded to sell back to a London publisher. And shortly before the book itself came on the market, the author received some advance publicity when *Life* magazine ran an editorial referring to "Parkinson's Law (after nobody)" — assuming that the name was a pseudonym. In the next issue *Life* printed our letter of correction, which pointed out that C. Northcote Parkinson, Raffles Professor of History at the University of Malaya in Singapore, might resent the statement that he did not exist. The first of many books by the learned professor, it has added a useful phrase to the language.

English trips were not confined to London. In Yorkshire I spent a wet weekend with John Braine, best remembered — like many novelists — for his first book, *Room at the Top*. John and his wife were as cordial as the weather was dour. Long evenings in crowded pubs, a visit to the Brontës' Haworth Parsonage, a solitary walk (John stayed in the pub) over barren moors that evoked the setting of *Wuthering Heights*. More exhilarating, if not much drier, was Susie's and my trip to Peter Scott's Wildfowl Trust at Slimbridge in Gloucestershire — the final destination of a fortnight's journey by canoe on the English canals and the River Avon.

These random samplings from visits to England all have to do with the years following World War II. Another early incident may be worth mentioning, as a sidelight on those two close friends, Gilbert Winant and Winston Churchill, both of whom would become Houghton Mifflin authors. One summer morning in 1945, when I was in London with the Office of War Information, I had returned directly to my office in Grosvenor Square from a weekend's fly fishing on the River Test, one of those famous chalk streams. I was wearing an old tweed jacket, pants worse for wear, and boots to match. Precisely at noon the telephone rang: "This is the Ambassador's office. The Ambassador would like to know if you can come for lunch." Obviously Mr. Winant wanted to talk about the autobiography he was writing for HMCo; I pointed out that I couldn't do private business while I was working for the government. "That's all right, he just wants to talk with you." So off I went to his residence in South Audley Street, around the corner from the Square. Cordial greetings, no one else there, and from the start it was clear that he wanted an audience more than advice. In the course of the one-way conversation he recalled how he had first heard of the attack on Pearl Harbor. Sunday, December 7, 1941, 9:00 P.M. He and Averill Harriman were visiting the Prime Minister at Chequers. As they sat around the supper table, Churchill turned on a small portable radio that Harry Hopkins had given him as a sort of advance Christmas present, and they listened rather sleepily to the nine o'clock news. Suddenly word came of the Japanese attack on Pearl Harbor. According to Winant, Churchill wanted to declare war on Japan immediately; Winant had to remind him that this required a meeting of the House of Commons. (Churchill's version in his memoirs is slightly different: "I got up from the table and walked through the hall to the office, which was always at work. I asked for a call to the President. The Ambassador followed me out, and, imagining I was about to take some irrevocable step, said, 'Don't you think you'd better get confirmation first?'")

Winant was a rather Lincolnesque figure, tall, lanky, apparently shy, and short of words in public, which I don't suppose was intentionally attention-getting, but which certainly served that purpose. This was evident when, later on, he spoke about his book at the Houghton Mifflin sales conference. But with a one-man audience the flow of words was nonstop. He reminded me of Thomas Wolfe as he strode around his London living room, stripping off his jacket and vest and loosening his tie. From time to time I stole a look at my wrist watch; there had been no mention of lunch. Finally, at 1:55 I thanked him and took my leave, ran around the block to the American officers' mess in the Grosvenor Hotel, and squeezed in as the doors were closing at two o'clock. Such was my "lunch" with the Ambassador.

Winant's end was tragic, and puzzling. The day before his book was to come off press — he was then back at his home in Concord, New Hampshire — he had asked his friend Henry Laughlin to send him an advance copy by special delivery, since he wanted to take it with him to New York, where he had a dinner engagement the following evening. The book was sent, and arrived on time. But Winant never saw it. While his secretary was at the post office picking it up, he took out a gun and shot himself.

When I came to Park Street we had a distinguished list of British authors, thanks in large measure to F.G., whose friendships overseas dated back to the years before the First World War. His knowledge of English literature was supplemented by his skill with the fly rod. It has been said that the British give as much devoted attention to the dry fly and the herbaceous border as the French do to the art of love. Greenslet shared his passion for trout fishing with John Buchan, Rafael Sabatini, and many others, including England's

Foreign Minister, Sir Edward Grey. But as he points out in *Under the Bridge*, the focus of interest in new writers began to shift in the nineteen thirties to this side of the Atlantic.

Though the center of American publishing had long since moved from Boston to New York, almost all the British publishers came here as well — ostensibly to visit Houghton Mifflin and Little, Brown, but also, I suspect, to decompress after a frantic fortnight in the metropolis and the horrors of too much steam heating. At our home in Lincoln, Susie and I were able to provide an antidote for both. In those days we had only a small unheated guest room, ever since known as the icebox. This suited Victor Gollancz and particularly his wife, Ruth: "At home I expect to wear the same costume indoors and out." Victor himself joined the HMCo list with his unique anthology, *Man and God*, a sort of spiritual counterpart to *The Practical Cogitator*. Of all the English publishers, he planned his American trips most meticulously, far in advance. Almost too far. One New York editor found this a bit tedious. Having been asked in November to make an appointment on a certain afternoon in January, he replied: "My dear Victor: So sorry. I have to attend a funeral on that day."

9
Building the List

E ditorial trips — whether to England or to areas west of Boston — were stimulating, exhausting, and occasionally fruitful. But the core of the operation lay in the daily routine at Two Park Street. In my time we had some three thousand manuscripts or book projects to deal with annually. Approximately ninety adult books were published each year. This was about the limit if we were to preserve a close personal contact with our authors. Even so, we occasionally failed to do so. There was never quite enough time. I remember thinking that one could spend a large part of the day simply keeping in touch with writers already on the list, quite apart from building for the future.

Procedures were pleasantly informal. The managing editor would assign each manuscript, as it came in, to one of the editors. If the first report was favorable, it might get two or three more readings. Those that survived this process would be discussed at a weekly conference which included, in addition to the editors, representatives of the sales and promotion departments. When a completed manuscript (or sometimes a project) was recommended for publication, a report by the editor-in-chief, including royalty terms, would be read to the next meeting of the company's board of directors or executive committee. I can recall no occasion on which such a recommendation was turned down.

These mechanical details, like the gear shift of a Model T Ford, are worth recording largely for their antiquarian interest. A later reorganization enlarged and increased the authority of the weekly Trade Department meetings; approval by higher authority became even more of a formality. The composition of the board of directors was changing. When I came on the board, all members but one were actively engaged in running the company: the Trade Department, the Educational Department, and the Riverside Press. Individual books might be discussed at some length. The proverbial fly on the wall would have had no doubt about what business we were in.

Official approval by the board of directors may some-times have been taken for granted. Not so approval by the sales force (and ultimately by the reading public). Consider the semiannual sales conference. Around the table sit the men and women whose job it will be to convince the wary, realistic, hard-shelled bookstore buyer — inured to publishers' rhetoric — to order an adequate advance supply of each title in the current catalogue. The duty of the editors is to provide them with the necessary ammunition. When the salesmen have already read and approved bound galleys, or when the author is well known, this can be easy. Presenting a new writer — a first novelist, for example — is more demanding. Eloquence is nice, but a good "sales handle" is better.

For a starry-eyed young editor, a sales conference is an educational experience. Suppose he reads and greatly enjoys a manuscript by an unknown writer. Should he recommend publication? Before making a decision, he imagines himself at the conference table, making his pitch to the skeptical salesmen. As Samuel Johnson said of a man about to be hanged, the prospect "concentrates his mind wonderfully."

So much for the mechanics. What of the fuel that kept the machine going? In the field of "nonfiction" — a negative term, but no one has found a better — we had a number of titles that still contribute heavily to the backlist. Here the Peterson *Field Guides*, mentioned earlier, were special in the sense that, while almost every title showed a rising curve of sales, the series as a whole has a life of its own, growing year by year. In the late thirties we published the first edition of Norman Taylor's *Garden Dictionary*. "Like your bank statement," wrote the garden editor of the *New York Times*, " 'The Garden Dictionary' is always right." Later it would appear, revised and enlarged, as *Taylor's Encyclopedia of Gardening*, and would spawn two small and handy offspring: guides to garden flowers and trees and shrubs — all of them in active use today. Speaking of guides, these were the days of FDR's New Deal and the Federal Writers' Project, one of whose outstanding products was the series of WPA guidebooks, of which the New England volumes were published at Park Street. In 1940 came the *Encyclopedia of World History*, a huge and hardy perennial by Harvard's William L. Langer and a team of historians. And the following year we brought out a book that was, so far as I know, a new departure for Houghton Mifflin: *The Natural Way to Draw* by Kimon Nicolaides of Chicago's Art Students' League. Starting with moderate sales, it has gone on forever — being the only book, I am told, the art teachers will use. (Other, I suppose, than their own.)

Another backlist item, forty years old as I write, is *The Practical Cogitator* by Charles P. Curtis and Ferris Greenslet — what the editors called "a sort of cerebral coast pilot," named after Nathaniel Bowditch's *Practical Navigator*. Only twice have I given a book a truly acid test. Once was during a canoe trip with Susie down the Connecticut River, when we were caught in a day-long downpour. Having no tent, we propped up one end of the canoe on crossed paddles, lay on our sleeping bags, and read out loud alternately from our only book:

E. B. White's *One Man's Meat* (published by Harper's). It was a happy day. Similarly, when I was in the hospital flat on my back after a spinal operation, I managed to hold the handy *Practical Cogitator* above my head for limited periods, between which I would mentally chew on the rich fare it provided. Not quite happy days, but a lot better than they would have been without that little book.

Henry Seidel Canby's *Thoreau*, for many years the standard biography, involved a shorter and somewhat ludicrous canoe trip: retracing part of Thoreau's famous excursion on the Concord and Merrimack Rivers. While I was driving around Concord with Dr. Canby, visiting spots associated with Thoreau, he remarked that he would like to repeat this 1839 excursion himself, as a background for his book. But when I suggested that my wife and I relieve him of this chore, he readily agreed. So we set forth from Concord on a sunny Saturday afternoon in July and by nightfall had reached the outskirts of Billerica, not far from where Henry Thoreau and his brother John camped on their first night out. Rain began to fall as we fought our way through the catbriars that lined the shore, till we reached an open space where we could sleep under the canoe. Premature firecrackers (this was July 3) punctured our repose. At dawn on the glorious fourth we discovered that we were not in "a place for fauns and satyrs" — as Henry describes their campsite — but in the town dump.

From Billerica the Thoreau brothers turned off on the Middlesex Canal, but since it had long ago dried up, we had to portage around a formidable mill-race before paddling downstream to the center of Lowell and thence up the Merrimack River, with highways resounding from both banks most of the way. By night-fall we had reached our objective: Nashua, New Hampshire. But how to get home? At length we found a broken-down taxi that took us and our boat back to Lincoln by 2:00 A.M. Here we learned that someone had reported to the Concord police seeing a couple in a canoe depart and not return. Presumably they were about to drag the river. On receiving my report of our journey, Dr. Canby decided that this was sufficient research for his purposes. I mention it merely as one small example of routine service by editors to their authors.

༄

At Park Street we have never been particularly strong at dreaming up a book project and then seeking a writer to carry it out. But sometimes we have been successful. One such example on our list was *Life in America*, published in 1951. I had read an illustrated article in *Life* magazine on the New England puritans and their concept of the world. The thought occurred to me that there might be a market for a new sort of history of our country, built around the ideas that have shaped it, as interpreted by contemporary artists and photographers.

I sought advice from Francis Henry Taylor, director of the Metropolitan Museum of Art. He did more than advise. He introduced me to his colleague Marshall B. Davidson, gave him a leave of absence, and thus allowed him full scope for his wide-ranging scholarship, his felicitous style, and his ability to blend pictures and prose in a single graphic narrative. When, five years later, Taylor wrote a foreword to the completed, two-volume work, he recalled Houghton Mifflin's original approach to the Museum in more elegant terms than it deserved: "The editors wished to produce a picture of American life as a whole — a picture composed of many pictures — which would glow with the somber integrity of an Eakins and ring with the joyousness of Whitman." We can claim no such aspiration. But it is a fair description of the finished book. This is what can happen when a writer makes an idea his own.

By no means all the Trade books originated in the editorial department. As they made their rounds, the salesmen became friends with booksellers all over the country and, through them, with local authors. Lee Barker, whose territory included the South and Southwest, was responsible for our publishing — among many others — the distinguished historian of the Western frontier, Walter Prescott Webb. The sales manager, Hardwick Moseley, brought us several successful writers, including Cornelia Otis Skinner; when he was a New York salesman, he had a part in steering the Churchill memoirs to Boston. The advertising manager,

Bob Linscott, developed close ties with the literary world, and later joined the editorial department. The publicity manager, Dale Warren, brought us Dorothy Thompson and later her close friend, Vincent Sheean. And some of the boldest projects were sponsored by the overall manager of the department. For instance, Lovell Thompson's long-time friendship with the artist, plus Lovell's readiness to take risks, resulted in *Andrew Wyeth,* an expensive volume that many booksellers viewed with skepticism. When the salesmen took advance orders in the spring, these skeptics suggested that we had gone slightly mad in printing so many copies. By fall they were furious at us for not having printed more.

All very well, you say; these are fine examples of the wool-bearing sheep, but how about the goats? Measured by sales alone, there were plenty of them on every list. But in defiance of natural laws (this was before the days of genetic engineering), some of these apparent goats later developed into very distinguished sheep. This happened most often, of course, in the field of fiction. But before I turn to that, I must mention one project that looked, in some ways, even riskier than *Andrew Wyeth* and involved not only the Trade Department but the company as a whole.

The *American Heritage Dictionary* was born in the brain of James Parton, a former editor of the *Harvard Lampoon*, who had become president of the American Heritage Company in New York. Jim, like so many others, took a dim view of the third edition of the unabridged *Webster*. Purporting to record the language as it was currently used, it tended to ignore syntax and established usage. In short, anything goes. He believed that American Heritage, in partnership with Houghton Mifflin, could do better. The initial investment was staggering. But under the direction of William Morris — widely experienced editor of dictionaries and author of books on words — and with imaginative layout and illustration provided by Heritage's H. Stanley Thompson, the new dictionary quickly found a place in the sun. Nor has it just basked there. It has provided offspring of every shape and size, which require a separate department of the company to take care of them. What I personally like best about the *American Heritage Dictionary* is its information on word origins. And I enjoy serving on the Usage Panel — not from my association with HMCo, but as a writer.

In my experience, the "creative" aspects of an editor's job, though essential, are limited. One can occasionally match an idea with a writer, but even so this is generally a logical extension of some theme with which he is already concerned, the recognition of a proven potential. A case in point is that of Bernard De Voto, who was one of the most distinguished, volcanic, and generous-minded authors on the Houghton Mifflin list. Though he lived nearby in Cambridge and was a friend of several members of the editorial staff, he came to us by an odd and circuitous route. Sometime in the early nineteen forties, a collection of watercolors by a little-known artist named Alfred Jacob Miller was discovered in a Baltimore museum: the only on-the-spot paintings of the early fur trappers, the Rocky Mountains, and the plains Indians of the Far West. A writer and literary agent, Emery Reves, had obtained publication rights and had approached De Voto — an authority on the American West — to write captions for a picture book. Impressed by the quality of the color reproductions in *Audubon's America*, Reves brought the project to Park Street. We liked it, but we wanted to carry it a step further: to have De Voto write a full-length account of the fur trade era, illustrated by Miller. Result: *Across the Wide Missouri*, Pulitzer Prize winner and the definitive work on this period of our history.

I quote with some hesitation an overgenerous letter from Benny written shortly after publication:

> I'd like, for the record, to put down what I said to you the other day, that I had never supposed I had a fur trade book in me, that the idea was yours, not mine, and that I'm pleased, as pleased as I ever get to be with my work, by the result. I take it that part of the editorial or publishing function is to understand what a writer is capable of. It's ironical to realize that I wasn't your writer when you figured it out.

In book publishing one author leads to another. To take a single example: Benny De Voto was surely responsible, in part, for our publishing Arthur M.

Schlesinger, Jr. (whose great contributions in history and biography are still in midstream). Arthur, no doubt, had something to do with our acquisition of *American Capitalism* by John Kenneth Galbraith some thirty-five years ago; Ken's and Arthur's incredible record of production and influence continues to this day. And through De Voto we acquired Garrett Mattingly's classic *The Armada*.

Not that Benny took his publishers too seriously. He began one letter to Mattingly:

Dear Mat: The Houghton Mifflin editors are as usual today, scattered over New England and the moose moors of Canada. That would be as usual favorable, except that . . . none of the secretaries who run the place are there. But I finally located Lovell Thompson, banding birds in Ipswich Bay . . . but [he said] hold everything till Paul Brooks returns from whatever identification with Thoreau he is currently engaged in . . . Meanwhile, go ahead and do what you damn well want to.

In presenting forthcoming publications to a sales conference, one is tempted to refer to a "well-balanced list." Presumably this implies careful planning. In fact, a season's list consists of a group of books, each chosen on its individual merits, which are currently in process of manufacture. For some mysterious reason, this group generally turns out (or did in my time) to be divided approximately fifty-fifty between fiction and nonfiction. The former would perhaps contain more candidates for immediate returns, the latter the greater contribution to the company's backlist. Many authors, of course, operated in both fields. Among them were Esther Forbes, Wallace Stegner, Charles Bracelen Flood, John Howard Griffin, John Dos Passos, Paul Theroux, and, on one occasion, John Kenneth Galbraith. Others consistently made the fiction best-seller lists: Ben Ames Williams, Anya Seton, Stuart Cloete, Lloyd C. Douglas, and — currently maintaining his high standard — Louis Auchincloss. And at least one poet, James Dickey, wrote a highly successful novel. But enough of names; at best this is a random selection among the scores of novelists who helped to keep our operation afloat. If I have seemed to deal summarily with them, as compared to writers and book projects in the field of nonfiction, that is because with novelists the editor's role, while essential, is too various and subtle to generalize about. Fortunately, there was a broad range of literary tastes among our editorial staff. Yet unlike Sir Stanley Unwin, we made plenty of mistakes.

Poetry — classified, rather awkwardly, under "fiction" — added quality rather than sales potential to the list. Archibald MacLeish appeared over our imprint for more than forty years. Elizabeth Bishop won a Literary Fellowship poetry award for her *North and South*. More recently, we published, among others, Anne Sexton and Galway Kinnell and, in a lighter vein,

Helen Bevington and Felicia Lamport. From John Murray in London came the work of the late poet laureate, John Betjeman.

Writers like these — and others too numerous to mention here — exemplify what I said earlier about the author-editor relationship. Each of them might well be the subject of a separate chapter. Take, for example, that dynamic trio: Benny De Voto, Arthur Schlesinger, Ken Galbraith. The last two, still active on our list, are among the most eloquent interpreters of the present age: each in turn has been a mainstay of the Park Street ship. For Arthur, who continues to write of even recent events with the long perspective of the historian, further comment would be premature. In Ken's case, the author himself has fortunately dealt with the subject so thoroughly and engagingly that to add another voice would be both inartistic and redundant. As for Benny, the full story has been admirably told, in a biography and a volume of letters, by the one writer most competent to do so, Wallace Stegner.

10
The Churchill
Memoirs

Probably the largest single enterprise during my time at Park Street was the publication of Winston Churchill's six-volume *The Second World War*. How this came about is of some interest. Emery Reves, the New York agent mentioned earlier in connection with Bernard De Voto's *Across the Wide Missouri*, was a specialist in international affairs. During the war he had brought us a successful book, *The Story of a Secret State*, by a young leader of the Polish underground, Jan Karski. In the prewar years Reves, a Hungarian by birth, had acted as literary agent for a number of prominent political figures in England and on the continent: he had the original idea of copyrighting their speeches and syndicating them in newspapers and periodicals throughout Europe. A persistent man, he finally got to see Winston Churchill, then out of office and living by his pen. Give me a year, Reves said, and I will double your literary income. He did. When the war ended and Churchill could once more write for publication, he remembered Reves.

The story, as Reves tells it, is not lacking in drama. Somewhere in central Europe he received a cable from Churchill telling him that he and Lord Camrose (publisher of the *Daily Telegraph* and head of the Churchill Trust) had been chosen to sell the American publication rights of the war memoirs, on which Churchill was now engaged. Reves and Camrose were to meet on the maiden voyage of the *Queen Elizabeth*, sailing from Southampton at noon on the following day. When Reves got to Paris, all flights to London had been canceled because of fog. He hired a private plane and reached Heathrow airport some two hours before the ship was to sail. On the drive to Southampton in a rented car, the chauffeur was forced by the fog to slow up at every low spot on the road. By noon they had reached the outskirts of the city; the *Elizabeth*'s smokestacks were in sight. Late in arriving at the dock, which was already empty of passengers, Reves was rushed aboard by waiting policemen. Churchill had held the ship.

Emery Reves and Lord Camrose met for the first time on shipboard. Since Reves had experience in book publishing, he would handle the United States book rights; as a newspaper man, Camrose would handle periodical publication. When Reves arrived in our New

York office to give us the first offer of this as-yet-unwritten work (his authorization simply a cable signed "C") there was a sense of urgency; everything had to be settled before the return voyage of the *Queen Elizabeth* five days later. As rapidly as possible, we worked out an agreement with Reves, covering the entire five- (later to become six-) volume work. Henry Laughlin, then HMCo president, called a special directors' meeting to confirm the arrangement; the ship was to sail at midnight, that same day. Not surprisingly, some doubts were expressed at the meeting. After all, the advance against royalties was many times what we had ever paid before; the author was seventy-two years old; hardly a word had yet been written. But Henry pushed the project through (and thereafter made the Churchill memoirs his special concern). At four o'clock that afternoon, eight hours before the ship would sail, I telephoned Emery Reves at his New York office and told him the deal was on. Lord Camrose was then at *Life* magazine with Henry Luce, who wanted to handle book publication rights if they were still free. They were not.

৯৯

By the early spring of 1948 Mr. Churchill had virtually completed Volume I, *The Gathering Storm*. Publication was set for June 1; the Book-of-the-Month Club had made it their June selection. But our production schedule was dangerously tight. While on an editorial trip to London I began to get urgent cables from Henry Laughlin and Lovell Thompson, manager of the Trade Department. Final copy had not yet been received, and publication was only about ten weeks off. (Publishers generally like to receive copy six months or more before publication day.) The following extracts from a lengthy exchange of cables tell the story:

March 13: STARTING MAKEUP MARCH 29 SPEED VITAL INQUIRE EARLIEST POSSIBLE DATE ALL MAPS
HENRY LAUGHLIN

March 16: AUTHOR INSISTS ON READING PROOF . . . THEREFORE QUICKEST TO AIRMAIL OUR GALLEYS TO ME . . . CARTOGRAPHER IN BRIGHTON WITH NERVOUS BREAKDOWN MAPS WILL NOT BE READY FOR A MONTH . . . SHALL ENDEAVOR TO OBTAIN ROUGH MATERIAL AND SEND TO BOSTON FOR REDRAWING . . . BROOKS

March 19: URGE CARTOGRAPHER IMPROVE DATE ON FINAL MAPS . . . STOP SEND LAYOUT SHOWING WHERE MAPS APPEAR IN TEXT SO PAGINATION WILL NOT BE DELAYED LAUGHLIN

April 5: BOOK OF THE MONTH HAS TO MAKE DECISION PUBLICATION . . . PROGRESS NOW DEPENDS ON RECEIPT OF FINAL GALLEYS AND OK MAPS STOP CAN YOU CABLE MONDAY WHEN WE WILL RECEIVE LOVELL

April 5: EXTREMELY SERIOUS SITUATION IF ANY
FURTHER DELAY PUBLICATION CHURCHILL
BOOK AND HOPE SOMEHOW IT CAN BE AVERTED
HARRY SCHERMAN
[President, Book-of-the-Month Club]

April 5: FOLLOWING TELEGRAM JUST RECEIVED FROM
CHURCHILL [He was spending the weekend
at Windsor Castle.] QUOTE ON WEDNESDAY
WHEN I HOPE TO SEE YOU I SHALL GIVE YOU
THE TEXT WHICH YOU CAN IMMEDIATELY SET
UP IN GALLEY FORM STOP WITHIN A FORT-
NIGHT AFTER I WILL GIVE YOU THE ABSOLUTE
FINAL SO THAT YOU CAN GO INTO PAGINATION
I HOPE THIS WILL BE SATISFACTORY STOP AFTER
ALL YOU ARE NOT PUBLISHING TILL EARLY
JUNE UNQUOTE PLEASE CABLE EXACTLY WHAT
THIS WILL MEAN IN PRODUCTION AND PUBLICA-
TION SCHEDULE INCLUDING BOOK CLUB STOP
EXERTING ALL POSSIBLE PRESSURE

BROOKS

April 6: CHURCHILL SCHEDULE PROPOSED YOUR CABLE
APRIL FIVE REALLY PUTS US IN THE SOUP . . .
IF COPY NOW RECEIVED NOT FINAL WORLD
PUBLICATION SHOULD BE HELD STOP SINCE THIS
IS NOW IMPRACTICAL ONLY SOLUTION DELIVERY
FINAL GALLEYS TO YOU WEDNESDAY [I had
already made an appointment to see Mr.
Churchill at his home in Hyde Park Gate
and try to get the galleys from him.] BOOK

OF THE MONTH MUST HAVE PLATE DELIVERY
DATE TUESDAY STOP LOVE AND KISSES

                                        LOVELL

April 7:   WE HAVE EMERGED FROM SOUP HAVE DIS-
PATCHED TODAY VIA AMERICAN OVERSEAS AIR-
WAYS CORRECTED TEXT . . . I TOLD CHURCHILL
THAT WE WOULD PROCEED FULL SPEED WITH
MANUFACTURE . . . HE DOES NOT EXPECT TO SEE
FURTHER PROOFS . . . MAPS WILL BE OKAYED
AT CONFERENCE WITH MILITARY ADVISORS
FRIDAY AM LEAVING TODAY [on a bicycle trip
with Susie through the South of England]
BUT WILL KEEP IN TOUCH WITH LONDON BY
TELEPHONE   BROOKS

April 8:   VACATION EARNED MAKE IT GOOD SEE YOU SOON
                                        LOVELL

When I had called on Mr. Churchill that morning,
he had obviously realized that we couldn't wait any
longer. I was ushered into his bedroom, one wall of
which was covered by a huge painting of the House of
Commons. He was sitting up in bed (his work habits
were like Mark Twain's) in a Chinese flowered dressing
gown, the counterpane covered with wide-margined
galley proofs, including a multitude of additions and
corrections in his own hand. (He disliked reading
typewriting, and had a private printer put his words
directly into type.) He asked what I thought of his
book, which we had read earlier in rough galleys. I did

not find it difficult to express enthusiasm. And by good luck he dictated a cable to Dan Longwell, managing editor of *Life* magazine, while I sat at his bedside. "Mr. Brooks, is there anything you wish to say?" Indeed there was. When printing an article based on a book, *Life* sometimes failed to give full credit to the latter. I suggested that a box be included on the first page of the first installment of *The Gathering Storm*, crediting the book to be published by Houghton Mifflin Company. This later appeared, word-for-word as dictated by the author.

Mr. Churchill's unique method of composition was indirectly responsible for our receiving copy for the first volume in the nick of time. After a glass of port and some mention of his paintings — then on display at the Royal Academy — I departed happily with a huge bundle of corrected galleys. Our Boston office had arranged for them to go on a flight to New York later in the day, to be met there and rushed to the Riverside Press. But no sooner had they arrived by messenger at the London airport than I had a telephone call from an English customs officer. What was the contents of this package that was in such a rush? I explained that it contained the first volume of Mr. Churchill's war memoirs. "In that case," he replied, "it must have considerable intrinsic value. I am afraid that we must keep it in customs for six weeks for evaluation." Long pause. "But," I finally said, "these are just galley proofs [I omitted to say that they were covered with additions in Churchill's handwriting], and you and I know that proofs are of no value." Long pause. "In that case," he conceded, "I think we can let them through."

With "final copy" safely at the Riverside Press, one might assume that all would be smooth sailing from here on in. But hazards still lay ahead. Last-minute corrections, which the author called "overtakes," kept arriving in Boston by cable. To maintain the printing schedule, the first chapters had to go on press before the final chapters had been set in type. And "overtakes" were not all. One Friday morning, after I was back at Park Street, Mr. Churchill telephoned me from Chartwell, his country home in Kent, with a correction that simply *had* to be made: he found that he had done an injustice to one of the generals described in his narrative. Fortunately this chaper was not yet on press.

In producing this first volume of the memoirs, we had a rather unfair advantage over the English publisher, Cassels; during these immediately postwar years, printers in Great Britain were not able to make books so speedily, or with such attractive paper and binding, as printers could in America. So the American edition of *The Gathering Storm* preceded the English. When Mr. Churchill received the first copy he was delighted. In his words: "It opens like the wings of an angel!" In the long history of the Riverside Press, one is tempted to say that this was "their finest hour."

෪

I saw Mr. Churchill only twice thereafter. In 1949 when he was in Boston to address the MIT Convocation, Houghton Mifflin gave a luncheon for him at the Club of Odd Volumes, including directors and their wives, with Henry Laughlin as host. Our guest was genial and displayed an amazing talent for identifying vintage champagne. But he said little during the meal. (He had been known to sit through an entire dinner without saying a word.) When the table had been cleared, however, he arose to give a spontaneous and impressive talk, the long rolling periods always coming to a perfect conclusion. Later the wife of a director remarked to me: "Mr. Churchill is a very interesting man, but he hasn't much small talk, has he?"

The following spring, when Susie and I were in London, Mr. Churchill invited us to lunch at No. 10 Downing Street. The other guests were Colonel F. W. Deakin (chief of the editorial team who assisted with his memoirs), Walter Graeber (head of the Time-Life London office), and Mrs. Graeber. Churchill was feeling relaxed, with nothing to do till the House of Commons met in midafternoon. The conversation had turned to the partition of Germany and Berlin. Susie, speaking lightly, remarked, "Mr. Churchill, any intelligent housewife could have told you *that* wouldn't work." He was not offended, but neither was he amused (his humor, I suspect, was a one-way street). The happy result was to raise the level of social conversation to a long and eloquent defense of the decisions at Yalta and

Potsdam. After lunch we were given a tour that included the cabinet room and the prime minister's garden; later in the afternoon, at his invitation, we watched the session at the House of Commons from the visitors' gallery — where we were appalled by the boos and groans and heckling of speakers, which would not have been tolerated in any New England town meeting.

By this time Churchill had completed the final volume of his war memoirs, which had been appearing at approximately yearly intervals, each volume a best seller and a selection of the Book-of-the-Month Club. In retrospect, the extent of the work involved is amazing. He had, of course, a team of assistants to organize the mass of material. But the words are all his. What made this possible, I believe, is the fact that every order, every memorandum — everything he wrote or dictated during the war — was immediately printed by H.M. Stationery Office and filed for future reference. Thus the memoirs have a rare sense of immediacy. They reflect Churchill's thoughts, his actions, his very words as history unfolds — a history he himself did so much to shape.

Rachel Carson
and "Silent Spring"

O NE DAY in 1950 when I was in our New York office, Marie Rodell — literary agent for many of the best American nature writers — came to call. She was accompanied by a quiet, soft-spoken employee of the Fish and Wildlife Service named Rachel Carson. This was before Miss Carson had finished the manuscript of *The Sea Around Us*, which would be serialized in *The New Yorker* and later published by the Oxford University Press: the best seller that started her on the road to fame. We had never met, though I was aware of her first book, *Under the Sea Wind*, which Simon and Schuster had brought out immediately before Pearl Harbor. It had received little recognition beyond professional circles. To the public at large she was virtually unknown.

Mrs. Rodell and Miss Carson were seeking a publisher

for an impressive but expensive project: a collection of paintings by Louis Agassiz Fuertes (see chapter 7) of colorful South American and Abyssinian birds, with accompanying text. It was appealing, but financially impossible. However, I did have in mind a book idea for which I was seeking an author. Rosalind Wilson, an editor at Park Street who spent summers on Cape Cod, had been struck by the ignorance of many of her literary acquaintances about the creatures that lived on the seashore. Couldn't we find some literate scientist to produce a guide to seashore life?

The writer whom Marie Rodell had brought to our office appeared to be the perfect answer. Marie agreed, and Rachel was definitely interested. With her current work in progress almost completed, she was already looking ahead. "No writer," she later remarked, "can stand still. He continues to create or he perishes. Each task completed carries its own obligation to go on to something new." Before she and Marie left the office, the idea was beginning to take shape for the book which — after a long evolution — became *The Edge of the Sea*, published by HMCo in 1955.

As I later learned, Rachel Carson's life up to this time had been something of a struggle. Born in 1907, a year before .Roger Peterson, she had, like him, made her own way by her talent, persistence, and early awareness of what she wanted to do. She was going to be a writer. During her childhood on a farm in the lower Allegheny valley of Pennsylvania, she had acquired — thanks largely to her mother — an awareness of the beauty and mystery of the natural world. "I can remember no time when I wasn't interested in the out-of-doors and the whole world of nature." But writing came first. When with the aid of a scholarship she entered Pennsylvania College for Women (now Chatham College), she assumed that the way to become a writer was to major in English. But in her junior year, fascinated by a compulsory course in biology, she switched to that field. Had she abandoned her dream of a literary career? Only later on did she realize that, on the contrary, she had discovered what she wanted to write about.

With a graduate degree in zoology, Rachel became a part-time teacher at Johns Hopkins and at the University of Maryland. (The spokesman for the pesticides industry who in after years attacked her scientific background should be forced to read her master's thesis: "The Development of the Pronephros during the Embryonic and Early Larval Life of the Catfish" [*Ictalurus punctatus*].) In 1935 her father suddenly died; now she was the sole support of her mother and two orphaned nieces. Despite the Depression — and thanks to winning first place in a competitive examination — she landed a job with the Bureau of Fisheries (later the Fish and Wildlife Service) as a "junior aquatic biologist." By the time I met her in New York, she had become chief editor of their publications and their principal writer. Her two careers had merged.

The writing of *The Edge of the Sea* is a good example

of how an editor's idea may evolve in the mind of a writer into something far more interesting than what was originally conceived. Rachel's aim was "to take the seashore out of the category of scenery and make it come alive." As the writing progressed, she began to see this book as something other than a "guide." The seashore below high tide line, belonging (in her words) "now to the land, now to the sea, . . . demands every bit of adaptability living things can muster." It is "a place where the dramatic process of evolution can actually be observed." Simply giving the factual information about each creature was not enough — and made for dull reading. The solution, she decided, was to incorporate this information in the captions for the illustrations (provided by her friend Bob Hines, an artist with the Fish and Wildlife Service). The project now appeared in a very different light: a companion volume to *The Sea Around Us*. Like that book, it would give full scope to her literary style: the blend of beauty and scientific authority — and above all the sense of identification with her subject — that makes her work unique.

Rachel felt a spiritual as well as a physical closeness to the individual creatures about whom she wrote. As I later recalled when writing her biography:

If I myself had to choose a single revealing moment during a long friendship with her, it would be shortly after dusk one July evening at her Maine cottage, while she was working on *The Edge of the Sea*. We had spent an hour after supper examining minute sea creatures under her brightly lit binocular microscope: tube worms, rhythmically projecting and withdrawing their pink, fanlike tentacles in search of invisible food; tiny snails on fronds of seaweed; flowerlike hydroids; green sponges whose ancestry goes back to the earliest record of life on earth. At last we were finished. Then, pail and flashlight in hand, she stepped carefully over the kelp-covered rocks to return the living creatures to their home. This, I think, is what Albert Schweitzer (to whom *Silent Spring* is dedicated) meant by reverence for life. In one form or another it lies behind everything that Rachel Carson wrote.

ঙ

The Edge of the Sea was perhaps the book that gave Rachel the greatest pleasure, involving, as it did, spending happy hours in the tide pools near her Maine cottage, the sand beaches of the Carolina coast, the mangroves and coral reefs of Florida. Supported now by the royalties from its predecessor, *The Sea Around Us*, she was able to leave government service and devote full time to her own writing.

To most authors this would seem an ideal situation: an established reputation, freedom to choose one's own subject, publishers more than ready to contract for anything one wrote. It might have been assumed that her next book would be in a field that offered the same opportunities, the same joy in research, as did the others. Indeed she had such projects in mind. But it was not to be.

While working for the government, Rachel and her

scientific colleagues had become alarmed by the wide-spread use of DDT and other long-lasting poisons in so-called "agricultural control" programs. Immediately after the war, when these dangers had already been recognized, she had tried in vain to interest some magazine in an article on the subject. Now, seventeen years later, when spraying of pesticides and herbicides (some of them ten times as toxic as DDT) was causing whole-sale destruction of wildlife and its habitat and clearly endangering human life, she decided she had to speak out. The magazines had failed her. The only answer was a book.

Rachel tried to find someone else to write it; as she would later remark, she was not at heart a crusader. But at last she decided that if it were to be done, she would have to do it herself. Many of her strongest admirers questioned whether she could write a salable book on such a dreary subject. She shared their doubts, but she went ahead because she had to. "There would be no peace for me," she wrote to a friend, "if I kept silent."

It was a formidable task, involving medical and other scientific material from all over the world. Rachel needed no editor, but I was involved in a minor way in making the introductory chapters on all these revolting poisons as readable as possible, and also in supplying the title. The phrase "silent spring" came to my mind while reading the chapter on birds, in which Rachel quoted a letter from a bird lover in Wisconsin, where aerial spraying had been particularly severe: "Summer mornings are without bird song. . . It is tragic and I can't bear it."

Silent Spring was over four years in the making. It required a very different kind of research from her previous books. No longer the delights of the laboratories at Woods Hole or of the Maine rocks at low tide. Joy in the subject itself had to be replaced by a sense of almost religious dedication. And extraordinary courage: during the final years she was plagued with what she termed "a whole catalogue of illnesses." Also she knew very well that she would be attacked by the chemical industry, not simply because she was opposing indiscriminate use of poisons but — more fundamentally — because she had made clear the basic irresponsibility of an industrialized, technological society toward the natural world.

When the attack did come, it was probably as bitter and unscrupulous as anything of the sort since publication of Charles Darwin's *Origin of Species* a century before. Hundreds of thousands of dollars were spent by the chemical industry in an attempt to discredit the book and in maligning the author, who was described as an ignorant and hysterical woman who wanted to turn the earth over to the insects. As in the case of her two previous books, parts of *Silent Spring* were serialized in *The New Yorker* (the one magazine that supported her work) before book publication. The industry immediately launched its attack, in the press and on the air — thereby creating more publicity than Houghton

Mifflin could possibly have afforded. This was all to the good. More serious was the attempt by the Velsicol Corporation of Chicago, the principal manufacturers of chlordane, to stop book publication, on the grounds that a statement about this highly toxic chemical was inaccurate. Fortunately, a professor at the Harvard Medical School, who was also head of the State Police Chemical Laboratory and an expert on poisons, was kind enough to read the relevant passage. Miss Carson, he reported, was correct, and he would gladly go to the stand for us if we were sued. So we went ahead. With publication of the book, the attacks intensified, frequently on the basis of statements attributed to the author that she had never made. Meanwhile, as a direct result of the message in *Silent Spring*, President Kennedy set up a special panel of his Science Advisory Committee to study the problem. Its report was a complete vindication of her thesis.

Rachel herself was singularly unmoved by all this furor. And she was very modest about her accomplishment. As she wrote to a close friend when the manuscript was nearing completion: "The beauty of the living world I was trying to save has always been uppermost in my mind — that, and anger at the senseless, brutish things that were being done. . . Now I can believe I have at least helped a little. It would be unrealistic to believe one book could bring a complete change." It may have been unrealistic, but history has proved it true.

Silent Spring is given much of the credit for initiating the so-called environmental movement. In a broader sense this book will remain an assurance to writers that, in our overorganized and overmechanized age, individual initiative and courage still count — that change can be brought about not through incitement to war or violent revolution, but rather by altering the direction of our thinking about the world we live in.

Postscript

NOT LONG AFTER Rachel Carson's death, her literary executor asked me to write a biography incorporating samples of her finest work. Since — unlike my previous writing — this was clearly a full-time job, I decided to resign my editorial position in 1969, five years before the then-compulsory retirement age of sixty-five. The transition was a smooth one. My successor, Craig Wylie, had been a pillar of strength in the editorial department for more than two decades.

Now as I look back at Two Park Street wholly from the writer's point of view, I realize how fortunate I was to have had some part in maintaining so notable a tradition.